The Treaty

3

between the Federal Republic of Germany
and the People's Republic of Poland

Published by the Press and Information Office
of the Federal Government

Wiesbaden, 1971

Printed by Wiesbadener Graphische Betriebe GmbH, Wiesbaden

PUBLIC DOCUMENT
Printed in Germany, 1971

Table of Contents

I. The Treaty Instruments

II. Signing of the Treaty

III. Articles and Comments

IV. Chronology

I. The Treaty Instruments

Treaty between the Federal Republic of Germany and the People's Republic of Poland concerning the Basis for Normalizing their Mutual Relations

THE FEDERAL REPUBLIC OF GERMANY
AND
THE PEOPLE'S REPUBLIC OF POLAND

Considering that more than 25 years have passed since the end of the Second World War of which Poland became the first victim and which inflicted great suffering on the nations of Europe,

Conscious that in both countries a new generation has meanwhile grown up to whom a peaceful future should be secured,

Desiring to establish durable foundations for peaceful coexistence and the development of normal and good relations between them,

Anxious to strengthen peace and security in Europe,

Aware that the inviolability of frontiers and respect for the territorial integrity and sovereignty of all States in Europe within their present frontiers are a basic condition for peace,

Have agreed as follows:

7

Article I

(1) The Federal Republic of Germany and the People's Republic of Poland state in mutual agreement that the existing boundary line the course of which is laid down in Chapter IX of the Decisions of the Potsdam Conference of 2 August 1945 as running from the Baltic Sea immediately west of Swinemunde, and thence along the Oder River to the confluence of the western Neisse River and along the western Neisse to the Czechoslovak frontier, shall constitute the western State frontier of the People's Republic of Poland.

(2) They reaffirm the inviolability of their existing frontiers now and in the future and undertake to respect each other's territorial integrity without restriction.

(3) They declare that they have no territorial claims whatsoever against each other and that they will not assert such claims in the future.

Article II

(1) The Federal Republic of Germany and the People's Republic of Poland shall in their mutual relations as well as in matters of ensuring European and international security be guided by the purposes and principles embodied in the Charter of the United Nations.

(2) Accordingly they shall, pursuant to Articles 1 and 2 of the Charter of the United Nations, settle all their disputes exclusively by peaceful means and refrain from any threat or use of force in matters affecting European and international security and in their mutual relations.

Article III

(1) The Federal Republic of Germany and the People's Republic of Poland shall take further steps towards full normalization and a comprehensive development of their mutual relations of which the present Treaty shall form the solid foundation.

(2) They agree that a broadening of their co-operation in the sphere of economic, scientific, technological, cultural and other relations is in their mutual interest.

Article IV

The present Treaty shall not affect any bilateral or multilateral international arrangements previously concluded by either Contracting Party or concerning them.

Article V

The present Treaty is subject to ratification and shall enter into force on the date of exchange of the instruments of ratification which shall take place in Bonn.

In witness whereof, the Plenipotentiaries of the Contracting Parties have signed the present Treaty.

Done at Warsaw on December 7, 1970 in two originals, each in the German and Polish languages, both texts being equally authentic.

<table>
<tr><td>For the
Federal Republic
of Germany</td><td>For the
People's Republic
of Poland</td></tr>
<tr><td>*Willy Brandt*
Walter Scheel</td><td>*Józef Cyrankiewicz*
Stefan Jedrychowski</td></tr>
</table>

Text of Notes sent to the Three Western Powers

The Treaty between the Federal Republic of Germany and the People's Republic of Poland having been initialled on 18 November 1970, identical Notes Verbales were transmitted to the Ambassadors of the Three Western Powers in Bonn on 19 November 1970.

Below is the translated text of the Note Verbale transmitted to the Embassy of the United Kingdom of Great Britain and Northern Ireland:

German Federal
Foreign Office   Bonn, November 19, 1970

The German Federal Foreign Office presents its compliments to Her Britannic Majesty's Embassy and has the honour to communicate to the Embassy the following text of a note of today's date of the Government of the Federal Republic of Germany to the Government of the United Kingdom of Great Britain and Northern Ireland:

The Government of the Federal Republic of Germany has the honour to inform the Government of the United Kingdom of Great Britain and Northern Ireland of the attached text of a Treaty between the Federal Republic of Germany and the People's Republic of Poland concerning the Basis for Normalizing their Mutual Relations, which was initialled on the 18th of November, 1970 in Warsaw.

In the course of the negotiations which took place between the Government of the Federal Republic of Germany and the Government of the People's Republic of Poland concerning this Treaty, it was made clear by the

Federal Government that the Treaty between the Federal Republic of Germany and the People's Republic of Poland does not and cannot affect the rights and responsibilities of the French Republic, the United Kingdom of Great Britain and Northern Ireland, the Union of Soviet Socialist Republics, and the United States of America as reflected in the known treaties and agreements. The Federal Government further pointed out that it can act only in the name of the Federal Republic of Germany.

The Government of the French Republic and the Government of the United States of America have received identical notes.

The Federal Foreign Office avails itself of this opportunity to renew to Her Britannic Majesty's Embassy the assurances of its highest consideration.

The Notes of the Western Powers

On 19 November 1970 the Governments of the Three Western Powers in Bonn likewise handed over identical notes in reply to the Federal Government. Below is the text of the note transmitted by the Government of the United Kingdom of Great Britain and Northern Ireland:

Her Britannic Majesty's Embassy
Bonn   November 19, 1970

Her Britannic Majesty's Embassy present their compliments to the Federal Ministry for Foreign Affairs and, on the instructions of Her Majesty's Principal Secretary of State for Foreign and Commonwealth Affairs, have the honour to transmit the enclosed Note Verbale:

Her Majesty's Government in the United Kingdom have the honour to inform the Government of the Federal Republic of Germany that they have received the Note of the Government of the Federal Republic of Germany of the 19th of November, 1970, enclosing the text of the Treaty between the Federal Republic of Germany and the People's Republic of Poland concerning the Basis for Normalising their Mutual Relations, which was initialled on the 18th of November, 1970 in Warsaw and reading as follows:

"The Government of the Federal Republic of Germany has the honour to inform the Government of the United Kingdom of Great Britain and Northern Ireland of the attached text of a Treaty between the Federal Republic of Germany and the People's Republic of Poland concerning the Basis for Normalizing their Mutual Relations, which was initialled on the 18th of November, 1970 in Warsaw.

"In the course of the negotiations which took place between the Government of the Federal Republic of Germany and the Government of the People's Republic of Poland concerning this Treaty, it was made clear by the Federal Government that the Treaty between the Federal Republic of Germany and the People's Republic of Poland does not and cannot affect the rights and responsibilities of the French Republic, the United Kingdom of Great Britain and Northern Ireland, the Union of Soviet Socialist Republics, and the United States of America as reflected in the known treaties and agreements. The Federal Government further pointed out that it can act only in the name of the Federal Republic of Germany.

The Government of the French Republic and the Government of the United States of America have received identical Notes."

Her Majesty's Government note with approval the initialling of the Treaty. They share the position that the Treaty does not and cannot affect the rights and responsibilities of the Four Powers as reflected in the known treaties and agreements.

Her Britannic Majesty's Embassy avail themselves of this opportunity to renew to the Ministry the assurance of their highest consideration.

Information by the Government of the People's Republic of Poland

The Government of the People's Republic of Poland has communicated to the Federal Government the following information on measures for a solution of humanitarian problems:

1

In 1955 the Polish Government recommended the Polish Red Cross to conclude an agreement with the Red Cross of the Federal Republic of Germany on the reunion of families; under that agreement, roughly one quarter million people left Poland up to 1959. Between 1960 and 1969, an additional 150,000 people have departed from Poland under normal procedures. In carrying out measures to reunite families, the Polish Government has been guided above all by humanitarian motives. However, it could not, and still cannot, agree that its favourable attitude regarding

13

such reunions be exploited for the emigration of Polish nationals for employment purposes.

2

To this day, there have remained in Poland for various reasons (e.g., close ties with their place of birth) a certain number of persons of indisputable ethnic German origin and persons from mixed families whose predominant feeling over the past years has been that they belong to that ethnic group. The Polish Government still holds the view that any persons who owing to their indisputable ethnic German origin wish to leave for either of the two German States may do so subject to the laws and regulations applicable in Poland.

Furthermore, consideration will be given to the situation of mixed and separated families as well as to such cases of Polish nationals who, either because of their changed family situation or because they have changed their earlier decision, express the wish to be reunited with near relatives in the Federal Republic of Germany or in the German Democratic Republic.

3

The appropriate Polish authorities have not received anything like the number of applications from persons wishing to leave the country for the FRG as is maintained in the FRG. According to the inquiries so far made by the Polish authorities, some tens of thousands of people may fall under the criteria possibly entitling them to leaving Poland for the FRG or the GDR. The Polish Government will therefore issue appropriate instructions for careful examination of whether the applications submitted are justified, and for their early consideration.

14

The Polish Government will authorize the Polish Red Cross to receive from the Red Cross of the FRG lists of the persons whose applications are held by the German Red Cross in order that they may be compared with the lists held by the appropriate Polish authorities, and carefully examined.

4

Co-operation between the Polish Red Cross and the Red Cross of the FRG will be facilitated in any way necessary. The Polish Red Cross will be authorized to receive from the German Red Cross explanatory comments on the lists, and will inform the German Red Cross of the outcome of examinations by the Polish authorities of transmitted applications. The Polish Red Cross will further be authorized to consider jointly with the Red Cross of the FRG all practical questions that might arise from this action.

5

As regards the traffic of persons in connection with visits to relatives, the appropriate Polish authorities will, after the entry into force of the Treaty concerning the Basis for Normalizing Relations between the two States, apply the same principles as are customary with regard to other States of Western Europe.

Joint Communiqué on the Visit of the Federal Chancellor to Warsaw

At the invitation of the Chairman of the Council of Ministers of the People's Republic of Poland, Józef Cyrankiewicz, the Chancellor of the Federal Republic of Germany, Willy Brandt, paid an official visit to Warsaw from December 6—8, 1970. He was accompanied by the Federal Chancellor's Deputy and Federal Minister for Foreign Affairs, Walter Scheel, the State-Secretaries Egon Bahr, Conrad Ahlers and Georg Ferdinand Duckwitz, and a number of personalities eminent in the political, cultural and economic spheres.

On December 7, 1970, Federal Chancellor Brandt and Federal Foreign Minister Scheel, together with the Chairman of the Council of Ministers Cyrankiewicz and Foreign Minister Jedrychowski, signed the treaty between the Federal Republic of Germany and the People's Republic of Poland concerning the basis for normalizing their mutual relations.

During the visit a talk took place between the Federal Chancellor and the First Secretary of the Central Committee of the Polish United Workers' Party, Vladislav Gomulka. Federal Chancellor Willy Brandt and Federal Foreign Minister Scheel also had talks with the Chairman of the Council of Ministers, Józef Cyrankiewicz, and Foreign Minister Stefan Jedrychowski.

The personalities accompanying the Federal Chancellor had the opportunity to engage in talks with corresponding representatives on the Polish side.

The talks took place in an objective atmosphere and proved useful and fruitful.

Both sides put forward their points of view with complete clarity. They expressed their satisfaction at the signing of the treaty and stated that its realization should

16

write an end to the past and create the prior conditions for a turning-point in the relations between the two States. They agreed that directly after the treaty comes into force the Federal Republic of Germany and the People's Republic of Poland will establish diplomatic relations with one another.

In the view of both sides, the normalization process inaugurated with the signing of the treaty is to pave the way for the resolution of the problems still existing in the sphere of international and human relations.

Both sides have affirmed their determination, guided by the terms of the treaty signed by them, to take further steps towards the complete normalization and comprehensive development of their relations. This applies particularly in the economic, scientific, technological and cultural spheres.

In the process of the normalization a special role falls to the share of the young people of the two countries.

Both sides are agreed that, as a basis for the normalization of the relations between the Federal Republic of Germany and the People's Republic of Poland, the treaty signed is not only of great importance for both States but also represents a vital contribution towards détente in Europe.

Both sides engaged in a detailed exchange of views on a number of current problems connected with the present international situation. They declare their faith in the principle of the peaceful cooperation of countries for mutual advantage, irrespective of different orders of society. They advocate a further reduction of tensions and will encourage the preparation and successful prosecution of a conference on questions of security and cooperation in Europe.

Both sides regard it as desirable to continue at appropriate levels the exchange of views on questions of joint interest. In particular, they have decided to create institutional forms for the joint discussion of problems connected

17

with the extension of the economic cooperation between the two countries.

The Federal Chancellor of the Federal Republic of Germany, Willy Brandt, invited the Chairman of the Council of Ministers of the People's Republic of Poland, Józef Cyrankiewicz, to pay an official visit to the Federal Republic of Germany. This invitation was accepted; the date of the visit will be fixed later.

II. The Signing of the Treaty

Address made by the Federal Chancellor
from Warsaw on Television

On the occasion of the signing of the German-Polish treaty on December 7, 1970, Federal Chancellor Willy Brandt made the following speech relayed over all the radio and television stations of the Federal Republic of Germany:

My fellow-countrymen,

I am well aware that this has been a difficult journey to make, but it is one that will be of consequence for the future. The Warsaw treaty should write an end to the sufferings and sacrifices of an iniquitous past. It should build a bridge between the two States and their peoples. It should open the way to bringing divided families back together again and make frontiers less divisive.

That being said, it would not have been possible to sign this treaty without having earnestly examined one's conscience. We did not take this decision lightheartedly. We are haunted by memories, by frustrated hopes. But our conscience is clear, for we are convinced that, in order to achieve a European peace order, tensions must be eliminated, treaties on the renunciation of force observed, relations improved and suitable forms of cooperation found.

In the pursuit of these aims we have to start from what actually exists and from what has developed. This also applies in respect of Poland's western frontier. No one has compelled us to take this view; we have come of age. The point now is to prove that we have come of age and that we have the courage to acknowledge reality.

What I said when I spoke to you from Moscow holds good for the treaty with Poland also; it does not surrender anything that was not gambled away long ago, and gambled away not by us who hold and held political responsibility in

21

the Federal Republic of Germany but gambled away by a criminal régime, by National Socialism.

We must not forget that what the Polish nation had to suffer after 1939 was worse than anything else it had had to endure in the course of its history. This injustice has not remained without consequences.

Our nation too suffered great distress, especially our East German compatriots. We must be fair: the greatest sacrifices were made by those whose fathers, sons or brothers lost their lives, but next to them it is those who had to leave their homeland who paid the most harshly for the war.

I refuse to accept legends, whether German or Polish: it is impossible to write the history of the German East arbitrarily.

Our Polish partners know what I wish to tell you at home in all clearness: this treaty does not mean that we acknowledge injustice or justify acts of violence. It does not mean that we give legal force to subsequent expulsion.

Resentment is an affront to respect for the grief that laments what has been lost—lost "in anguish, war and, alas, in unquenched tears", as Andreas Gryphus, the Silesian, put in at the end of the Thirty Years' War. No one can escape this grief. We are distressed at what has been lost, and the hard-tried nation will respect our affliction.

For a long time to come, names like Auschwitz will be in the minds of both nations and will remind us that hell on earth is possible. We have experienced it. But this very experience compels us to tackle the problems of the future with resolution. Escape from reality creates dangerous illusions. I maintain, therefore, that to uphold this treaty, reconciliation and peace, is to accept German history in its entirety.

A clear consciousness of history does not tolerate unrealizable claims, nor does it tolerate those secret reservations

Immanuel Kant, the East Prussian, warns against in his essay "Towards Eternal Peace."

We must direct our gaze towards the future and see morals as a political force. We must break the chain of injustice. By doing so we pursue a policy not of surrender but of common sense.

This treaty between Poland and ourselves—a treaty, as the official title says, concerning the basis for normalizing their mutual relations—is not a substitute for a formal peace settlement. It does not affect the rights and responsibilities of the Four Powers with regard to Germany as a whole. It does not invalidate any contractual commitments previously assumed by either side.

I wish to make special mention of this because our active participation in the West European Communities and our firm place in the Atlantic Alliance naturally form the foundation from which we shall seek a new and better relationship with the peoples of Eastern Europe.

Not until we regard the treaty in this overall context does it become clear what it means for peace, for the divided German nation and for a united Europe, a Europe which can be created not by rhetorical speeches but only by resolute work.

Nothing is more important than the creation of a stable peace. There is no alternative. Peace is not possible without European solidarity. Everything that brings us closer to this goal will be a service to our nation and, above all, to posterity.

Speech by the Polish Prime Minister in the Palais of the Council of Ministers

After the Federal Chancellor has laid wreaths at the monument to the Unknown Warrior*) and at the memorial to the Warsaw ghetto and has paid a visit to the Chairman of the Council of Ministers of the People's Republic of Poland, Mr. Cyrankiewicz, at 12.30 p.m. in the Palais of the Polish Council of Ministers the Polish and German Heads of Government and the two Foreign Ministers sign the Treaty concerning the Basis for Normalizing their Mutual Relations.

After the signing of the treaty, at a Luncheon in the Council of Ministers' Palais the Chairman of the Council of Ministers, Józef Cyrankiewicz, makes the following speech:

Mr. Chancellor, Mr. Vice-Chancellor, Honoured Guests,

Today we have signed a treaty that is of fundamental importance for the relations between the People's Republic of Poland and the Federal Republic of Germany. Also supported as an act within the framework of the general détente in Europe it was awaited, and because of this détente it is an act of great value for the consolidation of peace and security in our continent.

May the future, both the near in which we ourselves can operate actively and also the more distant, confirm the durability, and thus also the historic role of the treaty, which concludes a certain phase in the historical develop-

*) In the Memorial Book at the Tomb of the Unknown Warrior, Willy Brandt wrote these words: "In memory of the dead of the Second World War and the victims of violence and injustice, in the hope of a lasting peace and solidarity among the nations of Europe."

ment of Europe and finally recognizes and sanctions the European realities as existing for a long time, in particular the western frontier laid down at Potsdam.

Mr. Chancellor, it is the moral obligation of our generation, a generation which has lived through the Second World War, that we do not leave as a legacy to this young generation any matters resulting from this war—even only ostensibly—that are not brought to an end or even smoulder and sometimes become the festering germs of further conflicts.

That, Mr. Chancellor, is how I understand the signatures we have today placed under this treaty in the name of our Governments and States.

The treaty is the fruit of long and stubborn efforts. In the course of the activity, the good will on both sides had to overcome the problems—by no means so simple—that had accumulated in the past. In our efforts we have allowed ourselves to be guided by the conviction that in place of the previous wrong paths and beyond ravines, new ways are necessary and had to be built and opened together by filling in the gulf, so that in the process of the normalization of the relations between the two States the result will be a better understanding conducive, both for us and for the whole of Europe, to advantageous cooperation.

We allowed ourselves to be guided by the conviction that—if it is only in our power—the tragic chain of wars, suffering and injustice with which the history of Polish-German relations has been burdened up to now is finally broken, so that the gulf between the Polish and the German peoples that was torn by the hands of Hitler's barbaric intruders and occupiers in the period of the Second World War disappears.

The second German State, the direct neighbour of the People's Republic of Poland, the German Democratic Republic, twenty years ago, together with the People's Republic of Poland, signed the Görlitz Treaty which confirmed the Polish-German State frontier along the Oder and Lausitz Neisse laid down in the Potsdam Conclusions and helped to find a way to bridge this gulf.

This became the foundation of the process of normalization of the relations, the development of the peaceful cooperation, between Poland and the German Democratic Republic, not to speak of the alliance that is based on common ideological prerequisites—but that is naturally another matter.

And only on this basis, the recognition of the inevitability and inviolability of Poland's western frontier along the Oder and the Lausitz Neisse laid down in the Potsdam Conclusions, has it been possible to sign today this treaty which pioneers the way to the normalization of the relations between Poland and the second German State which arose out of the ashes of the Third Reich—the Federal Republic of Germany.

It would appear that through the treaty signed today we are creating a real and solid basis for the process of normalizing the relations between our two States which is to embrace various spheres of life, in particular the stimulation of the economic, technological and cultural relations, for the well-understood benefit of both countries. We are also agreed that immediately after the treaty enters into force, diplomatic relations will be established between the People's Republic of Poland and the Federal Republic of Germany.

We hope, after the entry of the treaty into force, that, as was the case with the Moscow Treaty, a more intensive normalization process will be initiated without complications and inhibitions, and we believe that this is also the wish of your Government. We would also like to think that this important matter will also meet with the good will of all intelligent political forces in the Federal Republic, because any resistance to the treaty, and therefore to the perspectives it opens, would contradict in a striking manner the endeavour of the nations, the vitally necessary normalization of relations, détente and peace in Europe.

We see in the treaty a sign and a significant share in the normalization process for improving relations between the socialist countries and the Federal Republic of Germany which started with the important Moscow Treaty of August 12. We expect this process to be continued and also to include a normalization of relations with Czechoslovakia, about which the Chancellor has already spoken.

We believe that the framing, the normalization, of the relations between the two German States will be of fundamental importance and unusually advantageous for peace and cooperation in Europe, in the first place on the basis of respect for the independence and sovereignty of both countries, with full equality of status with all other countries. With the greatest conviction, therefore, we give the fullest support to the question of the early accession both of the Federal Republic of Germany and of the German Democratic Republic to the United Nations Organization.

Already throughout Europe and all over the world, the treaty we have signed today has been regarded as a new, important step towards overcoming the odium of the Cold War in a sphere so sensitive to peace as Europe. With this step, we are helping to remove one of the most prominent and potentially dangerous seats of tension and, at the same time, promoting the process of the rapprochement of countries of various social conceptions, signs of which have already for a long time been noticeable in our continent.

We are realizing the prior conditions for a general security and cooperation in Europe. We are convinced that there are further opportunities for cooperation in this great question, including also the preparation and execution of a European conference.

27

Poland's share in the development of the European peace order is characterized by the fundamental treaty of friendship and mutual aid with the Soviet Union and by treaties with other fraternal, socialist States, as well as by numerous initiatives towards strengthening the trends towards reducing tensions in our continent.

The basic idea behind our policy, all our actions, is the effort to promote relations in Europe on the principle of peaceful coexistence. The prior condition is the coexistence of peoples and States in peace, freed from the burdens of the past and all the present great differences. A prior condition is also cooperation on all sides, particularly in the economic sphere, which is indeed the material basis for the development of the relations in other spheres.

Mr. Chancellor, Honoured Guests, in signing the present treaty on the normalization of relations between our two countries we have realized something to which not only was prominence given by our country and for the activatation of which a new platform was created through the initiative of Vladislav Gomulka, who now heads our country. This initiative, which is rooted in Poland's consistent peace policy and accords with the vital interests of security and cooperation in Europe, prepared the way for the talks.

We are fully conscious of the significance of the fact that in the name of the Federal Republic of Germany the signature under the treaty is set by a man who already at the outset of his assumption of power recognized the infinite misfortune that can result for the people of Germany, the peoples of Europe and peace in the world, through fascism. We also appreciate the impression of good will and the eloquence of these political forces which have evolved and are today realizing the present orientation of the Federal Republic.

28

In this we appreciate, Mr. Chancellor, your personal influence and that of Mr. Foreign Minister, Walter Scheel.

The possibilities of peaceful cooperation between our countries results from the wording and the spirit of this treaty.

They will be realized by the Government and people of our countries with the awareness of the significance of the treaty and the historic responsibility it imposes on our two States, their Governments and their social forces.

I would like to drink a toast to the treaty we have signed today and to its full realization, to you, Mr. Chancellor, to Mr. Foreign Minister Scheel, and to all the guests who have accompanied you, Mr. Chancellor, here from the Federal Republic of Germany, to the peaceful coexistence and security of our continent, to the peace that is so necessary in the world.

After- Luncheon Speech by the Federal Chancellor

Federal Chancellor Willy Brandt replied with the following speech:

Mr. Prime Minister, Mr. First Secretary, Honoured Guests,

At the same time in the name of Foreign Minister Scheel and that of the ladies and gentlemen who are accompanying us, I thank you for the generous words with which you have welcomed us. I am convinced that with the treaty we have taken the right step at the right time.

I believe that all of us who are present here today have the feeling that this December 7, 1970, is a special day for both our nations. With the signing of the treaty we have undertaken to set a final stroke and at the same time have given the sign for a beginning. You, Mr. Prime Minister, have spoken frankly and seriously about the sentiments moving your countrymen today. You deserve that I too do not indulge in mere diplomatic phrases. For my countrymen and me too this is a day which awakens painful memories—memories of the untold suffering that was inflicted on your people, but also memories of the great sacrifice my people have had to make.

This is therefore a day not without cares. We are only now standing at the beginning of a new relationship. The treaty we have just signed deals honestly with the "basis of normalization".

In the time lying behind us there has been no lack of attempts to form a new basis for the relations between our two countries. Serious discussions eventuated after Vladislav Gomulka and I in the last two years started making candid public statements one after the other. Thus, on both sides we have promoted a development which, I am convinced, is beneficial to the relations between our peoples, which will harm no other country, and which can make peace in Europe, a lasting peace.

This attempt was made possible through the successful work of our two countries' delegations. At the same time, in the name of my friends Scheel and Duckwitz and on behalf of their staff, I would like to thank Foreign Minister Jedrychowski, Deputy Foreign Minister Winiewicz and all the members of the Polish delegation for their share in the efforts which have helped to solve the difficult problems.

Normalization includes not only, but nevertheless also, the form. With satisfaction I would like to confirm our agreement to establish full diplomatic relations immediately after the treaty between our two countries enters into force.

30

The policy of my Government is directed towards an effective détente in Europe, above all in Central Europe. For this, the treaty of Moscow you, Mr. Prime Minister, have mentioned was a milestone. For this, the treaty signed here today in Warsaw is a decisive milestone. For this, is a treaty with Czechoslovakia, also. For this, is the contractually binding settlement of the relations between the Federal Republic of Germany and the German Democratic Republic.

But all this would be incomplete if there were no agreement on an improvement of the relations in and around Berlin — and of this from my own experience I could tell a pretty story. Time after time tensions in and around Berlin have developed. Viewed politically, I regard these individual different treaties and agreements as a whole in which each individual part has its own and indispensable place.

It will signify no hesitation if after the work on these treaties we direct greater energy to the questions of European security, the lessening of the armaments burdens, the balanced reduction of troops and economic cooperation. This will keep more than one conference busy.

In the centuries of our being neighbours, Germans and Poles have followed their road through history. It was a difficult road and the years following 1939 were incomparably the darkest stretch. Nothing can wipe this out. And yet I hope that we, supported by the lessons of history, can again make firmer contact, with the inevitably long process leading to mutual advantage, of giving and taking.

Mr. Prime Minister, Ladies and Gentlemen, I know that through today's act we cannot fill in the rifts that were so brutally torn open, and I also know that understanding, not to speak of reconciliation, cannot be generated by statesmen, but that they must mature in the hearts of the people themselves on both sides.

I hope that the treaty proves to be the strong bridge linking our countries and across which our peoples can come together, so that they can contact each other, can understand each other, and so that in the centre of Europe it gives an example of how antagonisms between East and West can be overcome.

My Government starts from what is. It accepts the events of history: conscience and insight lead us to conclusions without which we should not have come here.

But no one will expect me to undertake more in the political, legal and moral fields than accords with insight and conviction. Nor do we wish to belittle what results from the different situation of the two nations, from subscription to one or other security systems, from various social orders and political tenets.

And yet I believe that together we can achieve much if in the first place we realize this treaty in the direct sense and instil vitality into it, and in the second place if we place it in the service of security and cooperation in Europe. If this succeeds, then we have done a good job.

Mr. Prime Minister, I raise my glass to you, to the Polish Government and the Polish people, to the Council of State, to the First Secretary of the Polish United Workers' Party, to cooperation between our peoples, and to the young generation for whom we wish to secure a peaceful future.

After-Dinner Speech of the
Federal Chancellor at Castle Vilanov

At a Dinner in honour of the Chairman of the Council of Ministers of the People's Republic of Poland at Castle Vilanov on December 7, 1970, Federal Chancellor Willy Brandt made the following speech:

Mr. Prime Minister,
Your Excellencies,
Ladies and Gentlemen,

It gives me particular pleasure to be able to welcome here in Castle Vilanov both you, Mr. Gomulka and Mr. Cyrankiewicz, together with numerous personalities eminent in the public life of the People's Republic of Poland. I am also glad that the German guests who have accompanied me here have made a start, yesterday and today, on talks with their partners.

For me, as for the ladies and gentlemen accompanying me, the events of these days are very moving, although I know that we are only at the beginning of a new road.

I thank you very sincerely for your proverbial Polish hospitality and for the frankness with which we have been received. I am also grateful to all those who have prepared this visit such great care, however much it may fall outside the setting.

If I say that difficult problems remain to be solved I am fully aware of the inadequacy of this statement. It has its place in the more prosaic, occasionally formal, speech of the jurists and diplomats, but it does not reflect what the people are feeling, with you and with us. Nor do we wish to be silent about it at a ceremonious occasion.

I take up what the First Secretary of your United Workers' Party, Vladislav Gomulka, said in a speech a few days ago. He talked about a new phase and a new climate in the

33

relations between our two countries. And he said that this would favour practical cooperation in the scientific, technological and cultural spheres. You, Mr. Prime Minister, reaffirmed that at noon today. I fully agree. Here too we wish to remain realistic, but in point of fact there are wide fields for fruitful cooperation to our mutual advantage.

Allow me to say in this connection how important I consider it that many young people in our two countries should get to know one another. We in the Federal Republic of Germany wish for a European Youth Organization and we would be glad if the result would be a closer cooperation of the young people of our two countries. It is also for this reason that I asked representatives of our youth organizations to accompany me on this journey.

It will be a matter on both sides of according a prominent place in practice to the complex of human relations and reliefs. If we allow the people to come together, this can produce a great deal of good, not only for those immediately concerned but for our two countries as a whole.

I know that great psychological, political and legal problems are associated with this, but I am confident that you appreciate the importance of these tasks just as clearly as we do and that you will make great efforts to arrive at satisfactory and rapid solutions. At home I have often said: policy is made for people.

The cooperation in the economic and technological spheres will be very important, even if at the same time there should be no neglecting of the intellectual, scientific, educational, artistic and general cultural relations. If beyond all the vicissitudes of history two nations have lived in such close contact as we, they should not be afraid of snatching at the common elements of their cultural heritage positively and making them fruitful in their future relations.

34

Let me say quite openly and seriously: for many of my countrymen whose families have lived for generations in the East, today is a day overladen by special problems. Many feel as if it is only now that the loss they suffered 25 years ago is making itself felt. To a certain extent pipedreams were cherished. But I ask myself whether here in Poland too, wrongful ideas, that it was impossible ever to trust us in the Federal Republic of Germany, were not harboured. Time will still be required on both sides. But, like Abraham Lincoln, I think it is wise today to plant the tree that takes long to come to full flourishing.

If we direct our gaze towards the future I would like to ask that we declare our faith in what members of both our nations created before the inroad of barbarism. This persists, above all, in the realm of the intellect, and it persists in what, with effort and a respect of history, our nations have reconstructed. If we have the courage, the strength and the modesty to uphold this, then nothing is lost in the intellectual substance, and indeed in the end both our nations will profit thereby.

You may be sure we realize that this is no easier for you than it is for us. But that is just makes what the commonness of a fate from which there is no escape. There is only one way: the frontiers must be less divisive, less painful.

Let us summon our nations to follow the road that leads to one another and with one another. I recall more than one speech of Charles de Gaulle that referred not only to Germany and France but also to Germany and Poland. We were agreed that the peoples of Europe will find in their identity a great perspective for our continent.

The talks, not yet concluded, I have been able to engage in here in Warsaw have convinced me that the process of normalization, which has its firm foundation in our treaty, will continue to make progress. The well-known legal positions to which the Federal Republic of Germany remains committed need not stand in the way.

Just as you, honoured Polish guests, have your national interests in view, so do I contemplate a happy future for my own people. But I know that it is no longer possible to resolve our national problems in isolation but only on a European basis. This, too, has brought me here.

I raise my glass to you, Mr. Prime Minister, to all my guests and to the Polish nation, and, at the same time, to a happy future for both our peoples in a Europe lit by peaceful cooperation.

Statement made by the Federal Chancellor before the International Press in Warsaw

After the conclusions of his conversations, Federal Chancellor Willy Brandt made the following statement before the international Press at the Hotel Europejski in Warsaw on December 8, 1970:

The days in Warsaw are drawing to an end. For me myself and for many others they have been very moving. I have gained the impression from reports that the people at home in the Federal Republic of Germany have also found them moving.

How could it be otherwise? We have taken it upon ourselves to place the legacy of the war in such order that peace can be made more secure. This treaty we signed yesterday is the prior condition for an understanding and for better relations between the People's Republic of Poland and the Federal Republic of Germany.

This has once more become quite clear to me in my hour-long conversations with the leading men of the

Polish State. Equally as clear has been the appreciation that the two nations are seeking a new start, that they want to be good neighbours.

The treaty between the Federal Republic and Poland was not concluded by political parties but by responsible Governments. The Federal Government will be concerned to see that this treaty secures a political majority beyond political party limits. I am convinced that this is possible. At any rate I have been able to state that all democratic parties of our Federal Republic desire a settlement. Poland is ready to meet our good will half-way.

Today and yesterday we discussed a number of practical questions, in particular economic exchange and economic cooperation. This morning for this purpose Messrs. Beitz and Vetter also placed themselves at disposal with their advice. We have discussed cultural exchange and scientific and technological cooperation.

We have also with satisfaction taken note that the Red Cross societies in both countries are concerned to make good headway with matters for which they are to bear the responsibility.

For European politics the Warsaw treaty means a great deal. It should create a reasonable foundation for the cooperation urgently needed by future generations. It gives both States the possibility to make their policies clearer than hitherto.

That this is appreciated is shown by the reactions of our allies and the allies of our Polish partner to the treaty.

We still have a long way to go, but it will now be easier.

Statement of the Federal Chancellor after Returning from Warsaw

Federal Chancellor Willy Brandt made the following statement on his return from Warsaw on December 8, 1970, at the Cologne-Bonn airport:

I return home in the conviction that with the German-Polish treaty we have contributed something towards peace. This conviction helps to surmount painful memories.

To create a peaceful future we must overcome the past.

The Warsaw treaty is the foundation of a better understanding between Germans and Poles. It is also the means making it possible for many Germans who are still living in Poland to be reunited with their families, thereby assuaging much suffering that was a legacy of Hitler.

We are pursuing our policy for the sake of people, above all for the sake of the young people. They should never again find it necessary to have to grapple with the heritage of a criminal policy. We shall spare them that.

There is no alternative to what I call our peace policy. Nor is there any sensible alternative to this German-Polish treaty.

I am convinced that we shall be successful, beyond the political party limits, in securing a good political majority and I shall make this my concern.

III. Articles and Commentaries

The German-Polish Treaty

by Walter Scheel, Federal Minister for Foreign Affairs

Ever since the middle of the 18th century, the once so powerful and flourishing Polish State has increasingly fallen between the millstones of the old and new Great Powers in the East. Poland's history is one of Poland's partitionings. Repeatedly and over a long period, Poland's political existence was extinguished. The Third Reich even tried to annihilate the biological substance of the Polish nation and in any event wished to degrade it to the level of a Helot community.

Even the Polish State, resurrected after the Second World War, Polonia restituta, came into existence only after frontier shiftings and migrations of peoples. Not only did the burden fall upon Germans but upon millions of Poles as well.

No one can wonder that, after these experiences, the frontier question has plainly become the cardinal question for Poland. Every attack on the integrity of her national territory must be felt as an attack on her very existence. The trauma of having to be a "State on wheels" is very near the fear of non-existence. For Poland, the desire of every State for "secured frontiers" has a special significance.

Among the serious political forces in the Federal Republic of Germany there is scarcely anyone who is opposed to a German-Polish understanding and a reconciliation, who does not speak in favour of better relations, increased exchange, cooperation. Had this been possible, at the same time excluding the questions in dispute between the two nations, the Federal Government would have done so long ago. But things are not as simple as that. For Poland the mere renunciation of force for the securing of the future is not enough; it can help but little for the present, since Poland does not now feel herself threatened by the Federal Republic of Germany; nor she can feel herself so threatened.

Thus, anyone who wants the German-Polish understanding must immediately concern himself with the frontier question. He cannot sidestep this core of the German-Polish relationship. Anyone who does so sidestep it must take into account that there just can be no reconciliation, that this wide field must continue to lie fallow—with all the negative consequences it can have for peace and security in Europe. However, anyone who wants to "keep open" the frontier question under all circumstances must ask himself what he hopes to achieve if force as a means of changing frontiers is excluded in every respect. Neither now nor in any foreseeable future is a peaceful changing conceivable, since the Polish side will not find itself prepared voluntarily to hand over parts of its territory, and among our allies there is not one who would be prepared to influence the Poles on these lines. However, as far as the "keeping open" as a pledge, as a means to improve one's own negotiating position, is concerned, there could perhaps years ago have been an advantage in a "clear" recognition of the Oder-Neisse Line, as might also have been possible years ago, in normalizing relations with Poland without needing to bring up the frontier question. This possibility exists no longer. Time has not worked for us. The effect of "keeping open" is merely to obstruct every attempt to improve relations with Poland on a permanent basis. It is the denial of the future, the actual "fixation" of the negative aspects of the status quo, the guarantee that in our relations with the East nothing will change. Thereby, however, our relations with the West will also be conceivably burdened by mortgages which our West European partners, with whom we are seeking closer and closer ties, would hardly be prepared to assume. There can be no doubt that our "opening" towards the East not only does not hamper West European integration but first makes its progress possible. Vis-à-vis the East, however, and especially vis-à-vis Poland, what holds good is that if we cannot change the frontiers themselves we can make them easier to cross and in the long term make them unimportant, for in the final analysis it is not a matter of frontiers but of contacts between nations.

It is falsifying the problem if the Federal Government is accused of giving up or disposing over the German eastern territories. We cannot dispose over something that has long been at the disposal of history; we cannot give up something we no longer possess. To lose one's homeland is bitter; to look on Breslau, Danzig or Deutsch-Krone as Polish cities is bitter. But if at last after 25 years we take note of existing reality, it is not we who have created that reality. The Federal Republic of Germany has to shoulder the burden of the National Socialist legacy. No Federal Government can win the Second World War after it has taken place. For us, it can only be a matter of saying what is and seeing what can be made out of this reality and building on it.

However, this reality also includes the international, and certainly politically unique, situation in which Germany has found herself since 1945. In Germany, two States have come into being, but there is no peace settlement, and the Four Powers therefore continue to have rights and commitments with regard to Germany as a whole and to Berlin. The German States, which can speak only for themselves and, like other States, cannot act except with regard to their own existence, cannot make this peace settlement, which is still outstanding, superfluous by any action they may perform. If we say that, we do not harbour any chiliastic hopes; nor are we concerned solely with the unity of the German nation. We are thinking quite topically and quite concretely of, among other things, the links and connections that are vital for Berlin.

And for us there is yet another tie: by our signature we do not seek to legitimate injustice. No one has required of

43

us that we thereby associate ourselves with dubious historical theories. This, too, is a reason why the word "recognition" is not to be found in the German-Polish treaty. The Federal Republic of Germany is taking up a position it is not in her power to change. On the other hand, the treaty does not encroach upon the rights of German nationals. I have had it recorded in the minutes that we can neither contemplate nor agree to this.

These considerations have resulted in the treaty concluded in Warsaw. For the Polish side, its Article I is certainly the most important. In it, the Federal Republic of Germany has unequivocally undertaken not to place in question Poland's present western frontier. However, only on behalf of herself can she make such a declaration; she cannot bind an all-German sovereign State which does not yet exist; nor do we know when it will. Therefore, Article IV of the treaty, which deals with the continuing validity of existing treaties—and thus for the Bonn Conventions also—is of special importance; and this equally applies to the exchange of Notes between the Federal Republic of Germany and the Allies in connection with Article I, of which we have officially informed the Polish Government. Article I refers to what was laid down in the Potsdam Conference in the summer of 1945 and in the conference minutes. That is the source of the line taken by the frontier. The Article gives the Potsdam decisions no other nor added significance than results from the wording of the decisions and the circumstances under which they came about. Herein lies a vital distinction between this treaty and the Görlitz treaty concluded by the German Democratic Republic in 1950.

There has been much talk about the fact that a differentiation must be made between "frontier" and "line". I cannot agree. It is understandable that Germany's complicated situation since 1945 should have led to the origination of novel and extremely subtle legal definitions, but "frontier" means a point where a passport has to be produced.

In spite of this, the frontier article is not the only—and in a certain way not even the most important—article of the treaty. It merely creates the foundation for it. The German-Polish treaty is no frontier treaty, and even as an agreement on the renunciation of force it is only incompletely described. Its actual significance is depicted appositely as "treaty concerning the basis for normalizing relations". From the very beginning, both sides were clear that it was not in the first place a question of finding a "formula", but of initiating the normalization process. To this extent the German-Polish treaty is different from that concluded in Moscow, because, apart from the fundamental importance the frontier question now assumes in the relationship between Germany and Poland, between the Soviet Union and the Federal Republic there have for a long time existed relations which have first to be developed in the relationship with Poland. For this reason the Polish treaty could not, as the Moscow treaty, start with the renunciation of force as the essential core. Rather, the renunciation of force affirmed in Article II, the declaration of faith in the principles of the statutes of the United Nations, can form only one of the three elements upholding the treaty and one of two elements which are to be decisive for the framing of the relations.

Whereas the ban on force is self-explanatory, the actual counterpart to Article I is Article III. In it, both partners to the treaty undertake to initiate certain steps to normalize their relations fully and to develop them further. The purport of the Article is to open a clear perspective to the mutual relations. That is why we did not satisfy ourselves with the word "normalize"—with all that that implies—but we added the words "further steps" to make it clear that we visualize the development of the German-Polish

45

relations as a process that is not to be restricted to what is "normal" between any two States.

The task assigned to the two Governments in Article III requires execution. Quite certainly it will not be fulfilled at one stroke. The "normalization process" has already begun; even the talks that led to the conclusion of the treaty form part of it, just as do the economic treaty concluded in the meantime and the current negotiations on the consular powers of the missions on both sides. In other areas too, the improved climate has already loosened the fronts which for a long time had been completely rigid between the two countries.

But when we speak of normalization we think not only of economic or cultural exchange, of youth groups and orchestras. We would not have been able to conclude this treaty had we not had sufficient evidence that the Polish side was prepared to meet us halfway in the sphere of human reliefs for us decisive.

From the outset, this complex of problems formed a main theme of the negotiations in Warsaw. In its successful mastering we see not only the crucial test of the normalization but the fundamental complementation of the treaty as a whole. Even if this finds no formal expression in the treaty itself, it nevertheless forms a vital part of the instruments concerned in the German-Polish negotiations.

This was a matter of very difficult and delicate questions, not only for us but also for the Polish side. The Federal Government has always embraced them by the term "humanitarian sphere", at the same time being aware that this was only an inadequate description.

In the Federal Republic, this complex has often been described as the preservation of the "rights of people and groups". However, the Federal Government could not expect that the Polish side, by reason of its historical experiences, would already be prepared to bestow a

46

minority status on Germans living in Poland. It was from the standpoint of the Federal Government, too, to be remembered that the special rights of ethnic groups enjoyed by Germans in other Warsaw Pact countries are not based on such treaties and that they would certainly not have been possible had "protection" of the ethnic Germans been sought. In the negotiations it was a matter of finding pragmatic solutions by means of which the Federal Government could discharge the duties it has.

The "Information" the Polish Government has given us touches on themes of fundamental importance. It lies in the very nature of things that in it the emphasis is on the relatively easily comprehensible sphere of family reunion.

We know, however, that family reunion represents only one side of the problem and that the situation of the Germans remaining behind poses equally weighty questions. In the final analysis, both complexes are a matter of the normalization.

It would be completely false to regard the German-Polish treaty in isolation and statically. Rather, in it one must see the dynamic element contained in it, in the negotiations and in the normalization process. It is from there that the treaty gets its balance. To anyone who accuses us of luxuriating in future hopes it can be said that political treaties are always concluded only in the expectation of a particular political development and in order to promote the development and that they therefore can never be measured by the standards of a contract of sale and purchase determined by a concrete give and take.

It is said that Stalin wanted to create the Oder-Neisse Line as an eternal bone of contention between Germany and Poland. We have every reason to place this problem out of the area of controversy. With the treaty, we are inserting a fragment in the European peace order. We are aware that it is only a fragment.

47

On the Treaty with the People's Republic of Poland

I.

On November 18, 1970, in Warsaw, a treaty between the Federal Republic of Germany and the People's Republic of Poland concerning the basis for normalizing their mutual relations was initialled by the Foreign Ministers and was signed on December 7, 1970, in Warsaw, by the Heads of Government and the Foreign Ministers of the two countries.

The initialling of the treaty was preceded by six rounds of discussions at State-Secretary level between February and October and an intensive concluding phase of negotiations, headed by the Foreign Ministers, between November 3 and 14. These negotiations took place in a cordial atmosphere, with both sides demonstrating the wish to reach a successful outcome, with consideration taken of the two Governments' differing legal standpoints.

This conclusion was made possible by compromises on both sides. So far as was legally possible and with its contractual commitments preserved, the Federal Government complied with the wish of the Polish Government to place the frontier article in the foreground. In this connection the Federal Government started from the conviction that an agreement on a renunciation of force cannot by itself take sufficient account of the desire of the Polish people to live within secured frontiers, but that the road to a German-Polish understanding can be opened only by a simultaneous unequivocal declaration on the frontier.

For its part the Polish Government was prepared to accept the Federal Government's legal reservations regarding the frontier question as expressed in Article IV of the agreement and in the explanatory exchange of Notes. It was also prepared to take into account, within the scope of the normalization of the bilateral relations, the special significance attaching to the situation of the Germans remaining behind in Poland.

II.

The results achieved comprise, on the one hand, the initialled treaty. Its preamble registers the will of both States to overcome the past and create permanent bases of normal and good relations. In the treaty itself it is agreed that the Federal Republic of Germany and the People's Republic of Poland respect the existing boundary line as Poland's western frontier (Art. I), that they will allow themselves to be guided in their mutual relations by the principles of the peaceful settlement of disputes (Art. II) and that they will take further steps towards completing the normalization and comprehensive development of their mutual relations (Art. III).

In a further Article of this treaty (Art. IV) it is stated that this treaty does not affect international agreements previously concluded by, or affecting, the parties. The Federal Government has attached importance to this Article in order to make it clear that the Federal Republic of Germany can speak only for herself, that bilateral agreements between her and the People's Republic of Poland cannot be a substitute for a peace settlement for the whole of Germany, and that the rights and responsibilities of the Four Powers for Germany as a whole continue unchanged. An exchange of Notes on November 19, 1970, with the Governments of the Three Western Powers between the initialling and the signing serves to clarify this standpoint further. This exchange of Notes concerning the treaty was handed in at the Polish Foreign Ministry on November 20, 1970, by the head of our trade mission in Warsaw.

On the other hand, the outcome of the negotiations includes an understanding on the treatment of certain problems resulting after the Second World War from the expulsion of the majority of the German population and the placing of the East German provinces under Polish administration. In this connection, it is a matter in the first place of the question of the separated families and, on the other, of the situation of persons of German nationality who have, for various reasons, remained behind in Poland. There was a particularly intensive discussion of these questions in the final phase of the negotiations. We were from the outset clear that, by the very nature of the circumstances, they could—viewed from the Polish angle—scarcely be settled contractually. On the other hand, neither has the Polish side contested the existence of these problems and the need to solve them in the interest of the normalization of relations. In the end it proved possible on this basis to reach an understanding on how these problems should be treated. The Polish Government has informed us, in the form of a unilateral "Information," on the measures it intends to take. In particular, there is to be acceleration in the examination procedure of applications for resettlement, with the incorporation of the Red Cross societies and the inclusion of the applications received by the German Red Cross. The Polish delegation has assured us that the figure given on the basis of the particulars available at the present time to the Polish authorities are not to be interpreted as any final delimitation of the possibilities for resettlement. The conclusion of the treaty should also facilitate the visits of relatives in the two countries. We also hope—although this question is not touched on in the "Information"—that in the course of the normalization process it will also be possible to initiate linguistic and cultural reliefs for persons in Poland whose mother tongue is German.

III.

With regard to the legal significance and interpretation of the treaty, the following aspects are to be emphasized:

1. In the frontier question the Federal Republic of Germany binds herself in no way to any time limit.

Article I, Paragraph 1 of the treaty means that the Federal Republic no longer questions the Oder-Neisse Line as Poland's western frontier; nor does the Federal Republic make her own attitude dependent upon whether and when a peace settlement for Germany is realized in the future.

2. The declaration on the frontier question disregards the differing legal views of the two sides on the Potsdam Agreement.

In the Potsdam protocol the Oder-Neisse Line was taken as the boundary delimiting the territories placed under Polish administration, with at the same time a final definition of the German-Polish frontier being expressly reserved to a peace settlement. Therefore, the reference to the Potsdam decisions in Article I, Paragraph 1, says that in the relationship between the Federal Republic of Germany and the People's Republic of Poland this Line is in future to hold good as Poland's western frontier—i.e., from the entering of this treaty into force.

Moreover, the exchange of Notes with the Three Powers makes it clear that the rights and responsibilities of the Four Powers directly concerned with the Potsdam decisions are also unaffected.

Thereby the German side attaches to the Potsdam decisions themselves no other or deeper legal significance than results from the wording of these decisions and the circumstances that gave rise to them.

3. This treaty neither forestalls nor replaces a peace settlement.

As is seen from the explanatory exchange of Notes associated with the treaty, the Federal Government, in agreement with the Three Powers, made it clear during the negotiations that the rights and responsibilities of the Four Powers as expressed in the well-known treaties and agreements are not affected by the treaty. As is expressly stated in the Article 2 of the "Bonn Conventions," the reason for the continuance of these rights is the fact that no ruling on Germany in a peace settlement has yet eventuated. It is also seen from the Bonn Conventions that the rights and responsibilities of the Three Western Powers also apply to Berlin and Germany as a whole.

4. In the negotiations the Federal Government also made it clear that it can act only on behalf of the Federal Republic of Germany. This affirmation is also included in our Note to the Three Powers.

Thus, a reunified Germany cannot be bound by the treaty. In this sense, Article 7 of the Bonn Conventions retains its significance even if the Federal Republic states that, with the entering of the treaty into force, in the relationship between her and Poland the Oder-Neisse Line forms Poland's western frontier, and a dispute over the frontier no longer exists between the Federal Republic and Poland.

In any case, we attach fundamental importance, directed towards the preservation of the interests of Germany as a whole, to the formal maintenance of the reservation to a peace settlement.

IV.

In the negotiations we have stressed that through the conclusion of this treaty the Federal Government does not recognize as legitimate the expulsion of the German population and the measures associated thereby.

With the conclusion of the negotiations we have also emphasized that no one loses his rights as a result of the treaty under valid laws (e.g., nationality).

V.

All in all, we regard the results of the German-Polish negotiations as a balanced whole taking into consideration the interests of both States. The Federal Government hopes that these results will open the way to a progressive normalization of German-Polish relations. We believe that the Polish side also sincerely wishes for increasing cooperation in various areas.

We regard the agreement on the conclusion of a German-Polish treaty as a central part of our efforts to improve relations with the East European countries. We expect that this agreement will not only have a positive effect on our relations with the other East European States but will also exercise an influence for the better on the political climate in Europe generally.

On the Diplomatic History
of the Oder-Neisse Frontier (1939—1945)

by Hans Roos, Professor of East European History at the
Ruhr University, Bochum

In Article I, the frontier treaty between the Federal
Republic of Germany and the People's Republic of Poland
states that "the existing boundary line, the course of which
is laid down in Chapter IX of the Decisions of the Potsdam
Conference of 2 August 1945 . . . shall constitute the
western State frontier of the People's Republic of Poland". At
this Potsdam Conference, the Heads of Government of the
United States, Britain and the Soviet Union were agreed
that "pending the final determination of Poland's western
frontier" this frontier should run "from the Baltic Sea
immediately west of Swinemunde, and thence along the
Oder River to the confluence of the western Neisse River
and along the western Neisse to the Czechoslovak frontier". This representation of the frontier has now been
taken over in the present frontier treaty almost word for
word. This raises the question of the historical valuation
of the Potsdam frontier formula and its previous diplomatic
history during the Second World War. At the same time
it affects the problem of the historical relationship between
the Oder-Neisse frontier and the German-Polish frontiers
as existing on December 31, 1937. The principal features,
though by no means all details, have been clarified by
contemporary research inside and outside the Federal
Republic. The following survey can therefore give consideration only to the—to a certain extent—historically
substantiated features of the previous diplomatic history of
the Oder-Neisse frontier.

The first and most important preliminary condition for
the existence of the Oder-Neisse frontier lay in the policy
pursued by Adolf Hitler towards the Polish Republic,

particularly in the period immediately preceding the unleashing of the Second World War. Appended to the German-Polish non-aggression pact of August 23, 1939, was a "secret additional protocol" which defined the "spheres of influence" of Germany and the Soviet Union, in the event of Poland's military defeat, as being delimited by "approximately along the line of the Rivers Narev, Vistula and San". After the campaign in Poland and the invasion of Eastern Poland by Soviet troops (September 17, 1939), the Governments of Germany and the Soviet Union, in the Moscow negotiations of September 27—28, 1939, redefined their spheres of interest, which now—so far as Poland was concerned—ran along the Rivers Pissa, Narev, Bug and San. The German Government thereby assumed responsibility for almost the whole of the ethnically compact territory of the Polish population, and the Soviet Union received an area which, although it included some ethnically compact Polish districts—mainly around Bialystok—and scattered Polish settlement areas, contained on the whole a large White Ruthenian-Ukrainian majority. On November 1—2, 1939, the Supreme Soviets incorporated these territories, with the exception of the Vilna region, into the Soviet Union, thereby, in the view of the Soviet Government—which was, however, contested for a long time internationally—, founding the Soviet Union's constitutionally valid claim to these areas. Notwithstanding the fact that the continuity of the Polish Republic was still recognized by the Governments of France, Britain and the United States, the Soviet Union appealed to the referenda it carried out on October 22, 1939, in Eastern Poland, and thus to the right of nations to self-determination. The German Government did not employ the argument of self-determination for the area it occupied. By his decree of October 8, 1939, on "disposition and administration of the eastern territories", Hitler had about half the German sphere of interest, or about one-third of the Republic of

Poland in the frontiers as existing on December 20, 1937, attached directly to the German Reich. The area of the "Free City of Danzig" had already been attached to the Reich on September 1, 1939. With this drawing of frontiers, which existed factually from October, 1939, to January, 1945, Hitler for the first time departed publicly from the principle of the German-Polish frontiers as they were on December 31, 1937. He was able—at least for internal German consumption—to appeal to the doubtlessly correct facts that the German frontier with Poland had not been recognized voluntarily till then by any German Government. So far, the German Governments—particularly since the peace treaty of Versailles (June 28, 1919) and the Locarno treaties (October 16 and December 1, 1925)—had always made a quiet legal reservation that was to make a "revision" of Poland's western frontiers in favour of Germany possible. However, the Weimar Republic Governments had wished in any event to regain the territory of the "Polish Corridor" and Polish Upper Silesia, even if by no means all the areas inside the former frontiers of the German Reich as existing in 1914. On the other hand, with his annexation Hitler went far beyond the 1914 frontiers; this was justified neither by ethnic nor by historical claims. However, Hitler thereby also changed the character of the earlier German legal position, particularly vis-à-vis the Governments of France, Britain and the United States. These had examined extremely carefully the German legal reservation with regard to the German-Polish frontiers of December 31, 1937, and they had even in part supported, at least silently, the German demands for revision. Now the imperial wide-ranging foreign policy of the National Socialists destroyed every moral or legal claim which would have made a revision of the frontiers of December 31, 1937, possible, on, for example, the basis of the right of nations to self-determination. This nullified in every respect the thesis of the uncontested legal validity of the frontiers of December 31, 1937, as was propounded even immediately after the Second World War by large sections of the German population with complete subjective honesty but without a knowledge of the actual objective facts.

Hitler's action faced the British Government, which on March 31 and August 25, 1939, had guaranteed the existence of the Polish nation, with a very difficult choice; after all, it had to take the Soviet Government's standpoint into account. In reality the British Government had not, on March 31, 1939, guaranteed Poland's existing frontiers—the formula of August 25, 1939, ran somewhat differently—but the national integrity and the vital interests of the Polish nation. In doing so, the British statesmen had wished to keep open a reasonable frontier revision in favour of Germany which would be suited to prevent the outbreak of the Second World War. However, after the partitioning of Poland on November 28, 1939, this guarantee formula was also able to take the Soviet claims to Eastern Poland into account. Therefore, the British Foreign Secretary, Lord Halifax, on October 26, 1939, called public attention to the fact that "in essence" the new Soviet western frontier tallied with the frontier between Poland and Russia "recommended" by the British Foreign Secretary, Lord Curzon, on July 11, 1920. With this, Lord Halifax gave a line of demarcation, which had been originally conceived as an administrative boundary and an armistice line, the significance of a possible national frontier. This he was able to do with all the less concern as at the same time this "Curzon Line" represented approximately the eastern boundary of the ethnic population's compact settlements. With the German attack on the Soviet Union on June 22, 1941, which finally freed Britain from the danger of a German invasion, the British Government was more than ever obliged to take the Soviet point of view. Eventually, at the suggestion of the British Government, the Polish émigré Government then stationed in London agreed to sign a frontier agreement with the Soviet Govern-

57

ment on July 30, 1941; although this abrogated the German-Soviet partition treaties of August 23 and September 28, 1939, it in no way restored the old Polish-Soviet frontier *ipso jure*. Under these circumstances, Stalin was able to propose to the British Foreign Secretary, Mr. Eden, on December 16, 1941, in Moscow, that the Curzon Line should form the "basis of the future Russo-Polish frontier," at the same time suggesting that Poland be compensated at Germany's expense with, among other things, East Prussia. About two weeks previously Stalin had already proposed to the Polish Prime Minister, General Sikorski, that a "very slight alteration" should be made in the Soviet-Polish pre-war frontiers, in doing so mentioning "the Oder" as Poland's new western frontier on the lines of an adjustment. However, it remained uncertain whether he had meant the complete course of the river or only its upper course. Nevertheless, at a time when the German Armed Forces had suffered the decisive defeat at Moscow and the United States had entered the war, this is the first time that the idea of a "shifting of Poland westwards" and that of her "territorial compensation" at Germany's expense was formulated in diplomatic minutes. Sikorski himself did not fall in with this postulate of Stalin; in agreement with most Polish politicians and political parties, he merely wished that the future western frontier of Poland might be "straightened and shortened" at Germany's expense in order to guarantee Poland "the security she had deserved". Apart from this, it is highly probable that in December, 1942, he demanded a "natural security line" vis-à-vis Germany which should run "along the left bank of the Lausitz Neisse and the Oder including Stettin". There is no doubt, however, that Sikorski regarded this line not as a future frontier but merely as the delimitation of a future Polish zone of occupation which entailed no resettlement of the indigenous Polish population.

On April 25, 1943, because of the Katyn affair, the Soviet Government abruptly broke off diplomatic relations with the Polish émigré Government, which thereby ceased to be a partner with equal status in the territorial negotiations. Churchill at the time tried to get the Polish émigré Government to accept the Curzon Line, and this all the more as he already expected the émigré Government could soon "return to Poland" and that "free elections without pressure from outside" could take place. In view of the urgency of military decisions, President Roosevelt wanted decisions on questions concerning the European frontiers to be postponed until after the war, and for this he saw the appropriate instrument in the planned "United Nations". He recognized, however, the urgency of the Polish frontier question and therefore stated to Cordell Hull on October 8, 1943, that he was for a Polish-Soviet frontier that should run "somewhat to the east of the so-called Curzon Line", with "Poland receiving Lemberg". At the Teheran Conference (November 29 to December 1, 1943) Churchill proposed that "Poland could push forward towards the west like soldiers who with two paces 'close ranks to the left'". Eden was very impressed with Stalin's idea that "Poland could go west as far as the Oder". Finally, Roosevelt also agreed to a formula of Churchill, which was officially approved on December 1, 1943, and read as follows: "On principle, it is to be assumed that the home of the Polish State and the Polish nation should lie between the so-called Curzon Line and the line of the Oder and should include East Prussia (as defined) and embrace Oppeln". Thus, Poland's claim to a territorial compensation with Upper Silesia and Masuria was now already guaranteed, whereas the question of the other German territories east of the Oder had not yet been settled with complete unambiguity. Although the agreement of the "Big Three" had no binding force in international law, it was, all the same, in political respects decisive for the territorial form of Poland after the Second World War and thus for the establishment of the German-Polish frontiers.

On January 4, 1944, the Soviet armies crossed the Polish-Soviet pre-war frontier near Sarny and Rokitno and drew near the Curzon Line, thus making the frontier question an urgent problem. A further Soviet offensive, which started in White Ruthenia on June 21—23, 1944, in Volhynia and Eastern Galicia on July 17, 1944, and by the end of July, 1944, had brought Polish territory up to the Narev, the Vistula and the San under Soviet control, finally secured the predominant influence of Soviet politics in all questions affecting Poland. On July 22, 1944, a "Polish Council of National Liberation" was formed under Edward Osóbka-Moravski, which made its appearance, supported by the Soviet Government, as a counter-government in the country in opposition to the émigré Government in London. In its manifesto on principles, this so-called Lublin Committee advocated the attachment of Pomerania, Upper Silesia and Masuria to Poland and "Polish boundary-posts on the Oder", while accepting the Curzon Line, in principle, as a frontier in the east. The failure of the Warsaw uprising (August 1—October 2, 1944) and the course of the Moscow Conference (October 9—17, 1944) showed all too vividly how much the position of the London émigré Government had weakened compared with that of the Lublin Committee. At the Moscow Conference, the Polish Prime Minister, Stanislav Mikolajcyk, was unable to agree, in view of the attitude of most Polish politicians, to the called-for renunciation of all territories east of the Curzon Line, although Churchill put him under the "strongest pressure". On November 2, 1944, Churchill had him informed, through the so-called Cadogan Letter, that the British Government "would certainly advocate the advancing of the Polish frontier up to the Oder line, including the port of Stettin" and that it was prepared, together with the Soviet Government, to guarantee "the independence and integrity of the new Poland", even if the Government of the United States would not join in the guarantee. On November 17, 1944,

Roosevelt had Mikolajcyk informed that he would raise "no objections" to a frontier settlement agreed between Poland, the Soviet Union and Britain, although he could give "no guarantee for particular frontiers". Thereupon, on November 24, 1944, Mikolajcyk resigned, and from now on, although it remained formally in existence, the Polish Government no longer possessed any influence on the frontier settlement. On December 15, 1944, in the House of Commons, Churchill declared that "there never would have been a 'Lublin Committee'" had the émigré Government accepted the Curzon Line, and at the same time he indicated that he still believed in a social political constitution of Poland after the war, somewhere between the centre of western and eastern ideas. He therefore once more stated, on December 15, 1944, that Poland might receive "more than two hundred miles of Baltic coast" and that Poland was free, "as far as Russia and Britain were concerned", to extend her territory "westwards at Germany's expense".

The Yalta Conference (February 4—11, 1945) took place under completely different military and political conditions. On January 1, 1945, the Lublin Committee had been reorganized to form a "Provisional Government"; on January 12—14, 1945, the Soviet armies' great winter offensive started, with the Soviet Government's administrative control being extended westward, even during the Conference, beyond the frontier of December 31, 1937, bringing almost all regions east of the Oder and the Lausitz Neisse under Soviet control by March 10, 1945. Under these circumstances the British and American Foreign Secretaries, Messrs. Eden and Stettinius, on February 1, 1945, agreed that they "need not make the same concessions to the Lublin Poles" as they had previously "wished to make to Mikolajcyk". Now, they wanted to "keep their ideas in respect of the frontier along the Oder and Neisse fluid", especially as up to then the "western Neisse" had not been under discussion. At the same time they defined their demands for a "representative interim Government" and for "free elections" in Poland. Roosevelt and Churchill therefore rejected as too premature Molotov's proposal of February 7, 1945, that the western frontier of Poland should be fixed, with binding force, along a line "from Stettin (Polish) south along the Oder and further along the (western) Neisse". The "Big Three" finally agreed on a reorganization of the Provisional Government with the inclusion of certain émigré politicians as well as on a frontier formula that remained considerably behind the Teheran resolution: "The Three Governments consider that the eastern frontier of Poland should follow the Curzon Line, with digressions from it in some regions of five to eight kilometres in favour of Poland. They recognize that Poland must receive substantial accessions of territory in the north and west". The essence was the agreement that the "final delimitation of the western frontier of Poland should await the peace conference". Thus, a formula was found which was taken up again at the Potsdam Conference and, after the Potsdam Conference, was to form the basis of an international dispute about the significance of the Oder-Neisse frontier in international law.

After the Yalta Conference, the political antagonisms between the British and American Governments on the one hand and the Soviet Government on the other grew considerably more pronounced. On May 24, 1945, after it had several times announced its intention since February 5, 1945, the Polish Provisional Government officially placed the territories east of the Oder and the Neisse as well as the Free City of Danzig under its sovereignty. Then, on April 21, 1945, it immediately concluded a bilateral mutual assistance pact with the Soviet Government. The "Government of National Unity", constituted after much difficulty on June 28, 1945, gave members of the Provisional Government 12 out of 21 portfolios, including most of the key positions: apart from Osóbka-Moravski, Mikolajcyk and Gomulka made their appearance as Deputy Heads of Government with equal status. These acts gave the Western Governments the impression that a future peace conference would largely be prejudiced. On the other hand, already on April 13, 1945, the State Department had drawn the attention of the American President Truman—who had succeeded the now-deceased Roosevelt on April 12, 1945—to the fact that "the political stability and the maintenance of democratic governments" depended, especially in Germany, on a "minimum degree of economic stability". This consideration, to create a counterbalance to the Soviet sphere of influence now being developed, caused the American Government to revise earlier decisions concerning the political division of Germany, dismantling and reparation deliveries. The imminent completion of the atom bomb, the explosion of which did not, however, take place until July 21, 1945, also played a part in Truman's decision to pursue a harder policy against Stalin. Meanwhile, against the protest of Churchill, who had not been let into the secret about the atom bomb, Truman had the summit conference postponed from May to July, 1945, until the bomb was ready. However, as a result of its being completed too late, the atom bomb did not bring about a complete change in the "diplomatic balance" which Churchill, at any rate, had expected after he had been let into the secret. All the same, it is likely that the subsequent, unusually profound and long-lasting fear of the Governments of Poland and the Soviet Union of the United States' lead in the atomic field was due to the circumstance that the date of the completion of the American atomic weapon coincided with that of the Potsdam Conference.

Under these circumstances, the Potsdam Conference (July 17—August 2, 1945) resulted in a compromise in the Polish-German frontier question, a considerable part being played by the question of the political unity of Germany, the political constitution of Germany and Poland, and the economic stability of the two countries. The Three Heads of

Government "reaffirmed", on August 2, 1945, the agreement reached at Yalta, that "the final delimitation of the western frontier of Poland should await the peace settlement". The "former German territories" east of the Oder and the western Neisse, the southern part of East Prussia and also the "area of the former free city of Danzig" were placed under "the administration of the Polish State" and "for such purposes should not be considered as part of the Soviet Zone of occupation in Germany". Thus was found a formula which confirmed the already existing and—from the Eastern side partly anticipated—state of affairs without, however, possessing greater legal binding force than other political agreements. It is only in view of the fact that, for 25 years, the imminently expected peace conference has not yet taken place that the Potsdam formula became a subject of constitutional considerations which were, and are, unusually controversial. Thus, the Potsdam decisions were judged according to the respective political standpoints of the judgers in a way that fluctuated from its interpretation as a mere "declaration" via an "agreement" or an "arrangement" to a "preliminary peace". This lack of clarity was also due, to a considerable extent, to the fact that the Potsdam Conference could be interpreted an act of "ending the war" or of "undeclared peace", which was inapplicable in view of Hitler's "undeclared war". After all, the Government of National Socialist Germany had advanced and thus in every respect cancelled the frontiers of December 31, 1937—as long as they still actually existed—in a unilateral and illegal manner towards the east. Under these circumstances it was possible for the Polish western frontier along the Oder and the western Neisse, even if for 25 years it was formally something provisional, to become one of Europe's most durable and secure frontiers through the negative strength of the facts.

IV. Chronology

Chronology and Documents Relating to the Treaty with Poland

By Hans Ulrich Behn

July 17, 1945 to August 2, 1945

The Conference in Potsdam and the Potsdam Agreement

The Conference in Potsdam opens on July 17, 1945. Apart from the Heads of Government Stalin, Truman and Churchill (later Attlee), the participants include the Foreign Ministers of the Soviet Union, the United States and the United Kingdom.

The Conclusions of the Conference are made known on August 2, 1945, in the form of a final act as the "Potsdam Agreement". The Document is signed by the Heads of State/Heads of Government of the Great Powers participating in the Conference; the possibility of France's subsequent accession is envisaged. France declares her accession some weeks later and from September, 1945, is similarly bound by the Potsdam resolutions.

The Potsdam Agreement states:

In conformity with the agreement on Poland reached at the Crimea Conference the three Heads of Government have sought the opinion of the Polish Provisional Government of National Unity in regard to the accession of territory in the north and west which Poland should receive. The President of the National Council of Poland and members of the Polish Provisional Government of National Unity have been received at the Conference and have fully presented their views. The three Heads of Government reaffirm their opinion that the final delimitation of the western frontier of Poland should await the peace settlement.

The three Heads of Government agree that, pending the final determination of Poland's western frontier, the former German territories east of a line running from the Baltic Sea immediately west of Swinemunde, and thence along the Oder River to the confluence of the western Neisse River and along the western Neisse to the Czechoslovak frontier, including that portion of East Prussia not placed under the administration of the Union of Soviet Socialist Republics in accordance with the understanding reached at this Conference and including the area of the former free city of Danzig, shall be under the administration of the Polish State and for such purposes should not be considered as part of the Soviet Zone of occupation in Germany.

In addition, the Conference reaches the following agreement on the expulsion of the German population:

The three Governments, having considered the question in all its aspects, recognize that the transfer to Germany of German populations, or elements thereof, remaining in Poland, Czechoslovakia and Hungary, will have to be undertaken. They agree that any transfers that take place should be effected in an orderly and humane manner.

Since the influx of a large number of Germans into Germany would increase the burden already resting on the occupying authorities, they consider that the Allied Control Council in Germany should in the first instance examine the problem with special regard to the question of the equitable distribution of these Germans among the several zones of occupation. They are accordingly instructing their respective representatives on the Control Council to report to their Governments as soon as possible the extent to which such persons have already entered Germany from Poland, Czechoslovakia and Hungary, and to submit an estimate of the time and rate at which further transfers could be carried out, having regard to the present situation in Germany.

The Czechoslovak Government, the Polish Provisional Government and the Control Council in Hungary are at the same time being informed of the above, and are being requested meanwhile to suspend further expulsions pending the examination by the Governments concerned of the report from their representatives on the Control Council.

April 28, 1946

Polish Citizenship

The question of Polish citizenship for persons of Polish nationality living on the territory of the "retrieved areas" is legally settled. The Act comes into force on May 10, 1946. Article 1 of the Act "On Polish Citizenship for Persons of Polish Nationality Living on the Territory of the 'Retrieved Areas'" reads as follows:

Every person is entitled to Polish citizenship who was permanently domiciled in the territory of the "retrieved areas" before January 1, 1945, produces evidence of his Polish nationality before the Verification (Nationalities) Commission and on this basis receives confirmation of his Polish nationality from the competent authorities of the Public Administration of the First Instance and has taken the oath of allegiance to the nation and the Polish State.

Under Article 3 of an amendment to the Act, dated January 8, 1951, the competent authorities are empowered to recognize as citizens such persons as were domiciled in Poland since at least May 9, 1945, unless, as foreigners of a particular nationality, they had come to Poland and had been treated in Poland as foreigners. The recognition takes place *ex officio*. No application is required.

69

January 12, 1949

Administrative Attachment to Poland

The Polish Parliament enacts a law under which the former East German provinces are attached for administrative purposes to Poland.

September 20, 1949

First Considered View of the Federal Government on Poland's Western Frontier

In his first Government Policy Statement, Federal Chancellor Adenauer deals, among other things, with the question of Poland's western frontier (Excerpt):

The Potsdam Agreement includes the express statement: "The three Heads of Government—i.e., of the United States, the United Kingdom and Soviet Russia—reaffirm their opinion that the final delimination of the western frontier of Poland should await the peace settlement."

We cannot, therefore, under any circumstances tolerate a detachment of these territories undertaken unilaterally later by Soviet Russia and Poland.

This detachment contradicts not only the Potsdam Agreement; it also contradicts the Atlantic Charter of 1942 with which the Soviet Union has expressly associated herself.

The terms of the Atlantic Charter are quite unequivocal and clear. Through its Resolution of November 3, 1948, the General Assembly of the United Nations has invited the Great Powers to conclude peace settlements as soon as possible on the lines of these principles. We shall never cease in a proper legal procedure to pursue our claims to these areas . . .

We are entirely prepared to live in peace with our Eastern neighbours, especially with Soviet Russia and Poland. We most earnestly hope that the tensions at present existing between Soviet Russia and the Western Allies will be resolved in the course of time by peaceful means. But if I affirm our wish to live in peace with Soviet Russia, we assume that Soviet Russia and Poland, too, will allow us our right and allow our German countrymen, even in the Eastern Zone and in the part of Berlin that is under Soviet control, to lead a life in freedom corresponding to German tradition, German upbringing and German conviction.

June 6, 1950

Warsaw Declaration on the German-Polish Frontier

The Governments of the German Democratic Republic and the Polish Republic agree a joint "Declaration on the Demarcation of the Established and Existing German-Polish Frontier along the Oder and the Lausitz Neisse".

June 13, 1950

Considered View of the Bundestag
on the Warsaw Declaration

With the members of the Federal Government and the Bundesrat present, the German Bundestag assembles for a special session. The Senior Chairman, Paul Löbe, reads a joint declaration against the Warsaw Declaration of June 6, 1950 (Excerpt):

Ladies and Gentlemen, in the name of all Parliamentary Parties and groups of the Bundestag, with the exception of the Communist Parliamentary Party, and with the consent of the Federal Government and the Bundesrat, I make the following declaration:

In the agreement of June 6, 1950, signed by a delegation of the so-called Provisional Government of the German Democratic Republic and the Government of the Polish Republic, the assertion, untenable in international and political law, is made that a so-called peace frontier has been established between the Soviet-occupied Zone of Germany and Poland.

In conformity with the Potsdam Agreement, the German territory east of the Oder and Neisse, as part of the Soviet-occupied Zone of Germany, has been transferred to the Polish Republic only for provisional administration. The territory remains a part of Germany.

Ladies and Gentlemen, no one has the right to surrender land and people on his own authority or to pursue a policy of renunciation.

The settlement of this, as of all frontier questions of Germany, eastern as western, can be accomplished only through a peace treaty which must be concluded as quickly as possible with all nations by a democratically elected German Government as a treaty of friendship and good-neighbourliness . . .

July 6, 1950

Görlitz Agreement

In Görlitz, Otto Grotewohl and Georg Dertinger for the German Democratic Republic and Józef Cyrankiewicz and Stefan Wierblowski for Poland sign the Frontier Demarcation Agreement between Poland and the German Democratic Republic. In the Agreement the German Democratic Republic recognizes the Oder-Neisse Line as Poland's frontier:

The High Contracting Parties state unanimously that the established and existing frontier running from the Baltic Sea along the line west of the village of Swin-oujście and from there along the River Oder to the confluence of the Lausitz Neisse and along the Lausitz Neisse as far as the frontier with Czechoslovakia forms the frontier between Germany and Poland (Article 1).

August 5, 1950

Charter of the Persons Expelled from their Homeland

In the Charter of Germans Expelled from their Homeland, the East German Compatriots' Associations, assembled in Stuttgart, proclaim the expellees' basic views on expulsion and on the question of recovering their homeland.

They expressly renounce revenge and retaliation and affirm faith in a free, united Europe. They also call for the recognition of the right to a homeland as a God-given basic right.

The Charter reads as follows:

In the consciousness of their responsibility before God and man, in the consciousness that they belong to those who espouse Christian and occidental culture,

In the consciousness of their German national heritage, and in an appreciation of the common task of all European nations,

The elected representatives of millions of people expelled from their homeland have decided, after mature reflection and an examination of their conscience, to make a Solemn Declaration before the German people and the world at large laying down the duties and rights which the Germans who have been expelled from their homeland regard as their

73

Basic Law and as an indispensable precondition for bringing about a free and united Europe.

1. We people who have been expelled from our homeland renounce revenge and retaliation. We have come to this decision, for us solemn and absolutely earnest, in remembrance of the infinite suffering brought upon humanity, particularly in the last decade.

2. With all our energy we shall support every new start that is directed towards the creation of a united Europe in which nations can live without fear and violence.

3. Through hard, unflagging effort we shall participate in the reconstruction of Germany and Europe. We have lost our homeland. Homeless people are strangers on this earth. God has placed people within their homeland. To separate people from their homeland by force means the destruction of their spirit.

We ourselves have suffered and experienced this fate. We therefore feel ourselves called upon to demand that the right to one's homeland is recognized and is realized as a basic right bestowed by God on man.

As long as this right is not realized for us, we do not wish to be condemned to stand aside inactive, but, in new, improved forms, create and influence sympathetic and fraternal coexistence with all members of our nation.

Therefore, we claim and demand, today as yesterday:

1. The same right as citizens, not only before the law but also in the reality of everyday life.

2. A just and sensible distribution of the burdens of the last war over the entire German people and a conscientious execution of this basic principle.

3. The sensible inclusion of the Germans who have been expelled from their homeland in the reconstruction of Europe.

The nations of the world should recognize their responsibility for the fate of the people expelled from their homeland as the persons the most seriously affected by the sufferings of these times. The nations should act in the way that accords with their Christian duties and their conscience.

The nations must realize that the fate of the Germans expelled from their homeland, as that of all refugees, is a world problem the solution of which calls for the highest moral responsibility and an obligation to exert tremendous effort.

We call upon nations and people of good will to lend their hand to the work, so that out of guilt, misfortune, suffering, poverty and misery the way to a better future may be found for us all.

October 20, 1953

Federal Chancellor Adenauer on the Question of the German-Polish Frontier

During the third session of the Second German Bundestag, Federal Chancellor Adenauer refers to the question of the German-Polish frontier during his Government Policy Statement, in doing so also mentioning the question of a renunciation of force (Excerpt):

In conformity with the numerous declarations of the Bundestag, the German people will never recognize the so-called Oder-Neisse frontier. However, let me say one thing with the greatest emphasis:

The problems connected with the Oder-Neisse Line should not be solved by force but exclusively by peaceful means . . .

October 3, 1954

Statement by the Federal Government
on the Renunciation of Force

At the London Nine-Power Conference (September 28 to October 3, 1954) the Federal Republic declares her readiness to frame her policy in accordance with the principles of the statutes of the United Nations and to renounce any application of force.

The Federal Government makes the following statement about the minutes:

The Federal Republic of Germany has already stated her readiness to frame her policy in accordance with the principles of the statutes of the United Nations and accepts the obligations embodied in Article 2 of these statutes.

On the occasion of her accession to the North Atlantic Pact and the Brussels Treaty, the Federal Republic of Germany declares that she will abstain from all measures which are incompatible with the strongly defensive character of these two treaties. In particular, the Federal Republic of Germany undertakes never to bring about the reunification of Germany or the alteration of the present frontiers of the Federal Republic of Germany by violent means and to solve all points of controversy which may arise between the Federal Republic and other States by peaceful means.

February 18, 1955

Poland Lifts the State of War with Germany

After, on January 25, 1955, the Soviet Union—as the last of the four Occupying Powers—had announced that she regarded the state of war with Germany as ended, the Council of State of the People's Republic of Poland also decides to end the state of war between Poland and Germany. The Resolution reads as follows:

In view of the fact that 15 years have gone by since the attack made by Hitler Germany on Poland;

that after five years of war in which the Polish nation heroically fought against the Hitler occupiers, German militarism was crushed by the victory of the Union of Soviet Socialist Republics and the countries allied with her in the anti-Hitler coalition, thus creating the bases for the establishment of a lasting security in Europe and for a peaceful cooperation of the European peoples;

that the peaceful solution of the German problem lies in the vital interests of the Polish nation;

that the Government of the People's Republic of Poland has always supported efforts aimed at guaranteeing a peaceful stabilization of relations in Europe making impossible a revival of German militarism and the inclusion of West Germany in military blocs, a stabilization that is inseparably connected with the reunification of Germany on democratic and peaceful principles;

that the People's Republic of Poland has established friendly relations with the German Democratic Republic and is striving to make these relations still firmer;

that the People's Republic of Poland is striving to establish peaceful and good-neighbourly relations with the entire German people on the foundation of the peace frontier along the Oder and Lausitz Neisse, the Council of State resolves that:

1. The state of war between the People's Republic of Poland and Germany is regarded as ended.

2. Peaceful relations will be established between the People's Republic and Germany.

3. The People's Republic of Poland, acting in accordance with the rights and obligations resulting from the international agreements on the overcoming of the effects of the war with Germany, will continue her efforts directed towards bringing about a peaceful solution of the German problem, in the interests of peace and of the security of Poland and the other European nations.

December 8, 1955

Repatriation of Germans from Poland

The President of the German Red Cross, Herr Weitz, announces that the Polish Government has notified its consent to make it possible, from the beginning of 1956, for a monthly complement of from 800 to 1,000 Germans at present living in the Polish-occupied areas to resettle in the Federal Republic.

The Polish Government imposes no conditions and is prepared to bear the cost of transport to the frontier with the German Democratic Republic and to allow the people concerned to take movable property with them.

June 28, 1956

Considered View of the Federal Government on the Understanding with Eastern Europe

In a Government statement on the question of German-Polish relations during the 155th session of the Second German Bundestag, the Federal Minister for Foreign Affairs, Heinrich von Brentano, says, among other things:

The Federal Government does not think it is anticipating the Resolutions of a future all-German Government if, acting on behalf of the entire German people, it gives the assurance of the sincere desire for an understanding with the neighbouring peoples in Eastern Europe as well. The Federal Government thereby emphasizes the decisive principle guiding the whole of its foreign policy: to seek the solution of all contentious questions through peaceful agreements between free peoples whose coexistence is to be framed not by feelings of hatred, suspicion and retaliation but by the sincere desire for peace and common prosperity.

January 31, 1957

Federal Government Confirms its Attitude towards the Question of Germany's Eastern Frontier

In a Government statement during the 188th session of the Second German Bundestag, Federal Foreign Minister Brentano confirms the Federal Government's attitude towards the question of Germany's eastern frontier.

February 8, 1957

Considered View of the Polish Government

In expressing a considered view, the Polish Government emphasizes the inviolability of the Oder-Neisse frontier (Excerpt):

The frontier along the Oder and Neisse is, and remains, not only the inviolable peace frontier in Europe but also the basis of the lasting friendship and good-neighbourly cooperation between the People's Republic of Poland and the

German Democratic Republic. The inviolability of this frontier is guaranteed both by the unanimous and determined attitude of the Polish people and by the friendship linking Poland with the Union of Soviet Socialist Republics, the People's Republic of China and other socialist States, as also by appropriate treaties guaranteeing their common security. At the same time the Foreign Ministry of the People's Republic of Poland emphasizes that the Polish Government—in the conviction that this lies in the interest of all nations—will continue the policy of the normalization of relations and peaceful cooperation, irrespective of differences of systems, with all States who so wish.

June 15, 1957

Federal Chancellor Adenauer on the Possibility of an Improvement of the Relations

At a Press conference in Vienna on the occasion of his State Visit to Austria, Federal Chancellor Adenauer says that he, too, would be pleased if there were an improvement in German-Polish relations, although Gomulka and his collaborators were in a difficult position. For this reason one should do nothing that could be interpreted as an intervention in Poland's internal affairs or in relations between Poland and the Soviet Union.

September 22, 1957

The Federal Chancellor in a Television Interview

In a television interview with Columbia Broadcasting System (CBS) Federal Chancellor Adenauer confirms his standpoint on the question of the Oder-Neisse Line,

German-Polish relations and the right to one's homeland (Excerpt):

I have always said we shall never wage any kind of war on account of the Oder-Neisse Line, but I can very well imagine a development that leads to this question, too, finding a solution in a united Europe. I have always emphasized the right to a homeland, to the place where one was born. I have never said anything that goes beyond that. But if you just think about it, one day the whole of this region—Upper Silesia and so on—will have, in my opinion, to be in the European Coal and Steel Community, and equally in the Common Market, and the whole of the political frontiers we now have will increasingly lose their importance. Then with patience we shall have to seek a solution in the course of a general development.

September 24, 1957

Polish View on the Federal Chancellor's Interview

The central organ of the Polish United Workers' Party, "Trybuna Ludu", comments on the interview given by the Federal Chancellor to CBS (Excerpt):

... In this interview the true character of the assurances of Bonn Government circles on friendly feelings towards Poland was revealed. For his revisionistic conceptions Adenauer has found a new sign-board. He raises his claims not directly. His revenge-seeking programme is adorned with European feathers when he talks about the inclusion of the entire area behind the Oder-Neisse Line in the European Coal and Steel Community and the so-called Common Market. In point of fact, hidden behind this paraphrasing is the endeavour to change the present situation, the endeavour to undermine the territorial integrity of the Polish people and, in the final analysis, to wrench loose Poland's western territories . . .

January 10, 1959

Draft of Soviet Peace Treaty

To the Governments of the Federal Republic and the German Democratic Republic, the three Western Powers and other States who had taken part in the war against Germany, the Soviet Government transmits Notes for the summoning of a peace conference and the draft of a peace treaty with Germany.

In this draft treaty it says, in Article 8: "The frontiers of Germany will be as they were on January 1, 1959". In addition, pursuant to Article 9, Germany is "in conformity with the Potsdam Agreement of 1945" to renounce all rights, legal remedies and claims to the former German territories east of the Oder-Neisse Line.

January 18, 1959

View of the Federal Government

In an interview with the West German Radio, the Federal Minister for Foreign Affairs, Herr Brentano, describes the Soviet proposals as unacceptable (Excerpt):

There is no question of the right to re-order Germany's provisional territorial arrangement laid down in the Potsdam Agreement in a friendly talk with her neighbours with all coercion excluded. Germany is supposed to accept this unjust settlement without objection and finally . . . To these demands . . . there can be only one answer: a clear No.

August 31, 1959

Federal Chancellor Adenauer about the 20th Anniversary of the Start of the War

In an address broadcast on the eve of the 20th anniversary of the outbreak of the Second World War, Federal Chancellor Adenauer pleads for genuine friendship with Poland (Excerpt):

Twenty years ago, on September 1, 1939, the war started. Throughout long years, terror and violence prevailed in Europe, on the seas, in other parts of the earth. After the fighting has ceased the catastrophe of the terror was transformed into a period of dread, evoked by a rearmament more frightful and terrible than anything ever before seen by mankind. Not even yet, twenty years after, has true peace returned to the earth.

Today I will make no political speech, except that I would like to say that it must be the task of all people, whatever their belief, whatever their political views, to put an end to the state of unrest and armed fear, to bring back peace into the world that is filled by fear, so that all nations can devote themselves to genuine progress, within and without.

However, a special word must be said today about the first victims of the war through the invasion of the troops of Hitler Germany and the Soviet Union. I mean the Polish nation. For far more than a hundred years these kindly people, entirely blameless, suffered under the political and martial conflicts in Europe. Three times they were dismembered and partitioned, and twenty years ago they were the first victims of this last war when Hitler Germany and the Soviet Union swooped down upon the country and cruelly destroyed it.

The Germany of today is a Germany that is different from that under Hitler. The triumphal welcome that was prepared a few days ago for the victorious war-leader against Hitler Germany is evidence more striking than words of the profound change of feeling that today infuses Germans in comparison with National Socialism, its doctrine and its deeds. I say, therefore, that I am deeply convinced that this Germany, this new Germany, will one day be a good neighbour of Poland.

In the Second World War, in the concentration camp I found myself in company with Polish soldiers and officers. We were united by more than the fateful community of the concentration camp; in the camp we became a community upheld by a deep spiritual harmony.

In the last ten years, as Federal Chancellor of the Federal Republic of Germany I have often declared, and I repeat this declaration today, that it will be our endeavour to establish understanding, respect and sympathy between the Germany of today and the Polish people, so that on this soil one day true friendship may grow.

September 1, 1959

Comment of the Social Democratic Party of Germany

About the Federal Chancellor's speech, the SPD Press service writes, among other things (Excerpt):

Why does Adenauer talk about the future and writes a cheque out for it? Why does he not make a start right now? He makes no mention whatever of the present Government of Poland, Gomulka's Poland. Does he not consider it mature enough for the building of a bridge that hovers before his eyes? In the long years of his chancellorship Adenauer has directed his gaze exclusively towards the West. He has left Germany's immediate neighbours to the East completely on one side. His message to Poland on the anniversary of Hitler's onslaught, the product of external

necessities rather than of inner conviction, is scarcely likely
to make good the damage resulting from the twilight nature
of Bonn's official policy towards Poland.

November 21, 1959

Tenth Anniversary Celebrations of the Upper Silesia Compatriots' Association

In a speech on the occasion of the tenth anniversary cele-
brations of the Upper Silesia Compatriots' Association,
the State-Secretary of the Federal Ministry for All-German
Questions, Franz Thedieck, says, among other things, the
following:

The German legal claim compares with the Polish reality.
We should not be too ready to overlook this "new reality"—
to use the Polish slogan. Where up to 1945 more than ten
million Germans had their home, now something over seven
million people are living, only one-tenth of whom are German nationals or of German descent. This development, the
extent of the German disaster of 1945 and most certainly not
least the fault of those who in the German name wanted to
"organize" the Eastern area by extermination and the sup-
pression of foreign national characteristics—all this will
come to light in a peace treaty . . . We ourselves will have
carefully to turn possibilities of development over in our
minds and work out alternative solutions. Only with constructive ideas also taking into account the vital rights and
claims of our neighbours shall we be able to secure the
support and the good wishes of the partners to and signatory
powers of a future peace settlement.

July 10, 1960

Speech of the Federal Chancellor before the East Prussia Compatriots' Association

In a speech at a meeting of the East Prussia Compatriots' Association in Düsseldorf, Federal Chancellor Adenauer affirms the claim to the right of self-determination and expresses the hope that this right will one day hold good for East Prussia also.

July 20, 1960

Polish Note about the Frontier Question

The Polish Government believes it is able to conclude from the statements of the Federal Chancellor on July 10, 1960, that Adenauer can count on NATO support "in winning back Polish territory for Germany".

It therefore requests the Governments of the NATO countries, with the exception of the Federal Republic, to state their views on the present German-Polish frontier.

August 6, 1960

Declaration of the Compatriots' Associations about the Charter of the Persons Expelled from their Homeland of 1950

In Stuttgart-Bad Canstatt, on the tenth anniversary of the declaration of the Charter of the Germans Expelled from their Homeland, the President of the Expellees' League, Hans Krüger, makes the following supplementary declaration (Excerpt):

We affirm our faith . . . today, again and solemnly, in the fundamental principles listed ten years ago in the Charter of the Germans Expelled from their Homeland. For the sake of their realization we must now demand:

1. The right to self-determination guaranteed by international law and the statutes of the United Nations has to hold good for all nations, for the German nation as well. Its realization must not be sacrificed to the interests of other States.

2. We also recall that on June 5, 1945, the Occupying Powers formally affirmed that the division of Germany into four zones of occupation did not have the effect of an annexation. The Powers thereby made it clear that Germany cannot be partitioned nor German sovereign territory detached.

3. The restoration of Germany's unity is, therefore, not only a claim of the German nation secured by the right to self-determination but it also results from the aforementioned commitment of the Occupying Powers of June 5, 1945.

In these basic laws the Germans expelled from their homeland see the most important precondition for a lasting and happy peace in the world. Only in it can liberty and human dignity be maintained. To serve it is the mission of us all.

August 11, 1960

Western Powers' Reply to the Polish Note

In their replies to the Polish Note of July 20, 1960, the three Western Powers point out that under the Potsdam Agreement a final delimination of the frontier is reserved to a peace settlement and that the Federal Government has renounced in binding form the use of force.

October 19, 1960

**Note Circulated by the German Observer
with the United Nations**

In a Circular Note, the Federal Republic of Germany's Permanent Observer with the United Nations, Ambassador Knappstein, rejects Communist accusations against the Federal Republic. It is not true, he says, that the Federal Republic has illegally raised international tensions by putting forward territorial claims.

In the Note it says, among other things (Excerpt):

. . . 3. With reference to Poland's western frontier it was laid down in the Potsdam Agreement of August 2, 1945, that "pending the final delimitation" of this frontier of Poland the territories east of the Oder-Neisse were to be placed under Polish administration.

Thus, the Potsdam Agreement, which starts with the assumption that the frontiers of Germany are those as existing on December 31, 1937, has laid down an administrative boundary, not a frontier. The interpretation that the peace treaty to be concluded with Germany is to include only the formal recognition of this administrative boundary laid down in Potsdam was rejected at Potsdam by the Foreign Secretaries Byrnes and Bevin. In contrast, both Foreign Secretaries stated that with regard to Poland's western frontier the peace negotiations were not to be prejudiced by the Potsdam Agreement. In the October 10, 1945, session in the House of Commons, Foreign Secretary Bevin stated that the British Government was "in no way bound to support the existing provisional ruling of Poland's western frontier at the peace conference".

In conformity with this, on May 26, 1952, in the treaty governing the relationships of the Three Powers with the

Federal Republic of Germany, France, the United Kingdom and the United States agreed, in Article 7: "The Three Powers and the Federal Republic are agreed that it is an important aim of their common policy to reach a peaceful settlement for the whole of Germany on the basis of free agreements between Germany and her former enemies which are to be the basis of a lasting peace. They continue to agree that the final definition of the frontiers of Germany shall be postponed up to this date".

The peaceful demand for a final frontier to be determined in negotiations is thus in complete agreement with the texts quoted and is, therefore, valid in law. Apart from this, this political demand is fully in accordance with the principles of the United Nations on the renunciation of force in the event of international differences of opinions, the renunciation of threats of force within the scope of international relations, the recognition of and respect for sovereignty, the territorial integrity and political independence of States, and the readiness to refrain from any action which could heighten tensions.

June 14, 1961

Resolution of the Bundestag on Policy towards the East

The German Bundestag agrees to the following Motion of its Foreign Committee of May 31, 1961:

The Bundestag will resolve:

1. The Federal Government is invited to pursue, in company with its allies, a policy towards the East aimed at the restoration of a free all-Germany which maintains peaceful and flourishing relations also with the Soviet Union and all East European States.

89

In pursuit of this goal the Federal Government should seize every opportunity offered in order, without surrendering vital German interests, to achieve a normalization of relations between the Federal Republic and the East European States, seek to develop further the existing relations with these States in the economic, humanitarian, intellectual and cultural spheres, take into account in the framing of the relations with Poland the special psychological burdens inherent in the German-Polish relationship and, in the case of such countries as have deported parts of the German population or have German territory under provisional administration, insist on the respective necessary reservations in international law when establishing any possible official contacts.

2. The Federal Government is also invited to institute within the responsible Departments those institutional measures that offer the guarantee that both the entire complex of Eastern Europe and the development inside the individual East European countries can be dealt with in accordance with their significance. A report on the measures taken is to be made to the Committee for Foreign Affairs. With respect to the States and peoples of Eastern Europe the Federal Republic must be able to take political action that is carefully thought out and appropriate to the circumstances.

March 7, 1963

German-Polish Trade Agreement

In an interview with the German Press Agency (dpa), the Federal Minister for Foreign Affairs, Gerhard Schröder, states his views on the German-Polish trade agreement concluded the same day (Excerpt):

Question:

Mr. Minister, what importance do you attach to the German-Polish trade agreement concluded in Warsaw?

Answer:

In assessing the agreements signed in Warsaw one must, in my view, differentiate between various aspects:

First of all, here there has been a settlement of practical questions the solution of which lies in the interest of both countries. Lists of goods for German-Polish trade have been agreed, a protocol on shipping questions has been signed, and facilities have been created which are necessary for trade between the two countries to be carried on smoothly—namely, a Mixed Commission for the clarification and resolution of difficulties that may possibly crop up, and a German trade mission in Warsaw. With the institution of this trade mission something is created for German interests in Warsaw that, on the Polish side, has already been in existence with us for many years. In future, both Governments will be represented in the other country by a trade mission.

That is what I have to say about the technical side of the agreements. But that is only one aspect of the matter. If you take a somewhat deeper look at it, you cannot fail to recognize that a political significance also attaches to the conclusion of such an agreement dealing with various questions.

In this sense I would like to regard the agreement just signed as an important step on the road towards an improvement of our relations with Poland. We have expended a great deal of effort to realize this agreement. I mean that in doing so we have demonstrated good will. That must also be recognized on the Polish side. In this connection it is my especial hope that the open-mindedness and sincerity with which the negotiations have been carried out will also characterize, on both sides, the further framing of relations between Germany and Poland.

September 8, 1965

Federal Chancellor Erhard about the
German-Polish Relationship

In a statement on the theme "Understanding towards West and East", Federal Chancellor Erhard offers a settlement of all open questions:

The destiny of Germany and the destiny of Europe cannot be separated from one another. Nor without the unity of Germany will there be any unity of Europe. Where one tries to achieve a new order on the dismemberment of continents and nations which belong to one another through culture and history, one does not create peace but one allows unrest and uncertainty to continue. We know we have neighbours not only in the West but also in the East. We also know that our East European neighbours could not organize their relations with the German people according to their own wishes because they were dependent on Moscow in framing their foreign politics. If the demand for greater foreign political sovereignty continues in Eastern Europe, it is the task of European politics to make use of it. This will pose a threat to nobody; nor will the interests of the Soviet Union be compromised. We have established trade missions in some of these countries and we shall continue on this way. Only ourselves and not Pankow can represent Germany there.

For this reason our appearance must be made in Eastern Europe as well, since we consider it to be merely an illusion to think it is possible to solve the German problem against the wishes of the East European peoples.

I would like to address a particular word to our Polish neighbours. The respect I entertain for a great and valiant nation prevents me from believing that the Polish people think the alleged German thirst for revenge is a political reality. It just does not exist. More than renouncing revenge and retaliation—which the German expellees have done—, more than renouncing the use of force to secure one's rights, more than time and again holding out our hand for reconciliation—there is really nothing more one can do.

It is true that we reject many Polish theses and smearings which have once more been given an airing particularly in these last days in Breslau. In Warsaw, Mr. Haeckerup, the Danish Foreign Minister, has clearly stated with what simple means it is possible in the West to dispose of differences of opinions between countries—namely, by respecting the will of the people. Therefore, I repeat, here and now, that we seek a settlement of all open questions with all our direct neighbours which gives those concerned the feeling of security.

October 1, 1965

Protestant Memorandum on "The Situation of the Expellees and the Relationship between the German People and their Eastern Neighbours"

Preface

The Evangelical Church in Germany [i. e., the Protestant Church, the "EKD"], which, as an ecclesiastical community, is placed in the political field of tensions between East and West, is observing with growing anxiety that the wounds inflicted by the Second World War on the relationship between the German people and their neighbours in the East have not even yet, twenty years after the end of the war, scarcely begun to heal. On the German side a material reason for this is that the occupation by Soviet Russia and Poland of the German eastern territories on the far side of the Oder-Neisse Line and the expulsion of millions of Germans from these territories and from the old German settlement areas in Czechoslovakia and the rest of East and South-East Europe have raised problems to which it has not so far been possible to find an adequate solution . . .

Under the chairmanship of Professor D. Dr. Ludwig Raiser, Tübingen, the Chamber of the EKD for Public Responsibility has undertaken this task in the following Memorandum, which is published with the consent of the Council of the EKD. For the whole presentation, only the members of the Chamber coming from the Western member-Churches of the EKD are responsible . . .

Despite this restriction on the task, the Chamber, as the Council, has always been conscious that it is a question of problems of concern to the entire German nation. The solution of these problems is closely connected with the task of overcoming the most distressing cleavage of Germany.

I. Extent and Contexts of the Problems

Any contemplation of the situation of the expellees and the future relationship between the German people and their neighbours in the East must start by drawing attention to the extent of the human side of the disaster that has befallen the German East. In millions of cases the loss of homeland was accompanied by the loss of almost all external possessions, and also, in most cases, the loss of near relatives. Together with the fatigues of the expulsion and the struggle for naked existence, millions were faced with a complete crisis in their lives which also embraced the psychological, mental and spiritual substance . . .

The representation of the proceedings would be inappropriately shortened if, from the beginning, the human and historical fate of Germany's neighbours in the East was not also kept in mind . . .

The acts of injustice done to the Germans cannot be taken out of the context of the political and moral backslidings into which the German people allowed themselves to be led by National Socialism . . .

It must be described as particularly incriminating that, twenty years after the end of the Second World War, there are scarcely any signs of the possibility of engaging in an objective discussion of the momentous questions of guilt and justice between the peoples concerned . . .

Among the German people, too, time alone has not yet had a genuine healing and soothing effect on the human wounds and the political unrest caused by the expulsion. The more the assimilation of the expellees in State and Church appears outwardly to progress, the more obvious are the deeper-seated connections and results of the expulsion . . .

II. *The Expellees in Society and Church*

The fate of the expulsion has thrown fresh light on to the connection between people and their surroundings and perhaps has first made many of the persons concerned conscious of it. For this reason, the expellees have felt their fate to be not only a particularly devastating and wearisome crisis in their life, but it must be said that such loss of homeland, together with the destruction of all their binding and protective elements and the loss of possessions—at first appearing—and legal insecurity, signifies an all-embracing shock, a collapse of their previous basis of existence. With all that Church, State and Society have to say about problems of expellees, it must be remembered that in the case of the persons concerned the expulsion has resulted in an uncertainty in the relation to surroundings, a feeling of justice outraged, and a lack of confidence in the future . . .

III. On the Present Situation in the Territories on the Far Side of the Oder-Neisse Line

. . . Without doubt, here interests which no consideration can overlook have developed. Thus, already some years ago the then State-Secretary of the Federal Ministry for All-German Questions, Franz Thedieck, said: "Only with constructive ideas also taking into account the vital rights and claims of our neighbours shall we be able to secure the support and the good wishes of the partners to and signatory powers of a future peace settlement."

. . . The Polish Government, in declaration after declaration, is saying that the possession of the new Western territories is a vital necessity for the Polish people. It must also be noted that there is no difference in this matter between Communists and non-Communists, between State and Catholic Church.

IV. Questions in International Law

. . .

The investigation must start with the question as to whether in the case of the eastern territories a final change of territorial sovereignty has not already taken place and whether the expulsion of the German people who had been domiciled there was lawful. (These questions are answered in the negative. Ed.)

. . . Meanwhile, it would be premature at this place, as is so often the case, if this investigation were to be broken off with the assertion that only a complete restoration of the former state of affairs would satisfy violated rights. Whether and what compensation is to be demanded is, and remains, a matter for free political decision. However, before that decision is taken the German people must ask themselves the critical question whether they can, and will, indulge in the feeling of violated rights. After in the last war serious wrong was inflicted in their name on the peoples of the East, and in particular on the Poles who are now occupying and have resettled the territories, the German people must at the same time reflect what compensation they would require for the foreign rights they themselves violated . . .

Access to a legally satisfactory answer is blocked if the question is approached with the criminal law categories of guilt and punishment. International law recognizes no criminal law of the kind that the alleged collective guilt of a nation, or the guilt of its political leaders who had started a war and had acted unconstitutionally during this war, justifies the persons attacked from imposing sanctions at their own discretion as a punishment . . .

On the other hand, serious thought must be given to two other aspects. The one, Germany's neighbours in the East have reduced to the concept of an obligation on the Germans to secure peace; after her bitter historical experiences at the hands of Germany, the Polish State has an increased right to security and must therefore also be able to decide the frontiers which guarantee her the highest degree of security.

. . . In the German-Soviet Treaty of August 23, 1939 (Ribbentrop-Molotov Pact) the German Reich declared its approval of a new partitioning of Poland and the annexation of Eastern Poland by Soviet Russia. Therefore, a German Government must now hesitate to raise a legal claim to the return of territories the possession of which has become a vital economic necessity for Poland because of the loss of Eastern Poland . . .

A complete restoration of the old conditions of ownership, which might still have been possible in the first years after 1945, is now, twenty years later, impossible if thereby it would jeopardize Poland's existence, which Germany, after what has been said, must respect . . .

V. Theological and Ethical Considerations

... Even if the concept "right to one's homeland" has shown itself to be problematic, it nevertheless indicates legitimate values needing protection in the national system. A future re-ordering of the relations between the German people and their neighbours in the East will have to recognize this and not question the unjust character of what has happened. On the other hand, there must be no contemplation of right and its possibilities on lines that do not accord with history ...

... There will be no achieving of a future peace order without the German people also sacrificing old legal positions. The expulsion of the German population from the now Polish-administered and formerly German territories (the same naturally holds good for other areas as well) must be described as unjust and a violation of elementary moral precepts ...

Historical facts are best interpreted by describing the expulsion and the territorial changes as a compensation claimed by the Poles for their own losses and sufferings. However, just as little as these losses and sufferings must be denied or forgotten, just as little can "compensation" carried out arbitrarily nullify the wrongful character of the expulsion. At this point, here is substantiated part of the suffering by reason of which expellees plead for the "right to a homeland". On the other hand, no one who appreciates that it is simply impossible to restore the old state of affairs at any price objects to what has happened being placed on the political agenda ...

From this aspect, the Church too must object to a silent sanctioning of the expulsion by its recognition in a peace settlement. It must not be possible to overlook wrong inflicted by both sides on one another ...

VI. *The German Eastern Territories as a Political Task*

The examination of the constitutional and the theological-ethical aspects has shown that it is impossible to solve the problem of the German eastern territories by absolute arguments of right and ethics, by the means of a theology of the creation and history . . .

The matters here under dispute and all territorial changes require common contractual settlements. The value of these settlements depends on the mutual appreciation of their necessity and the mutual consent to make a new start . . .

Again, it is impossible in this Memorandum to detail the steps that can best promote the aim of reconciliation and reorganization. The only thing that is certain is that it is not enough rigidly and unilaterally to emphasize the German legal standpoint but that, on the other hand, no German Government can be expected to surrender its legal standpoint from the very beginning and unconditionally. Rather, it must first be a matter of creating an atmosphere among the German people themselves, and outwardly, in which, even in individual steps, acts of reconciliation with the neighbours in the East are then possible.

This assumes that also with these people a desire for reconciliation exists or can be awakened. They must therefore consider the critical question as to whether they wish to hold firm to their self-righteous attitude towards Germany they have so often ostentatiously displayed. But the discussion cannot be initiated until the German people have demonstrated that, for their part, they will resist the temptation to persist in their own self-righteousness.

November 18, 1965

Letter from the Polish Bishops to the German Bishops Assembled in Rome for the Council

During the Second Vatican Council in Rome, Polish bishops deliver to the German bishops a message intended to open the dialogue between the two nations. On the occasion of the millennium of Poland's Catholic Church, the Polish bishops describe Poland's thousand-year history, giving special consideration to the fact that Germany and Poland are neighbours and, in the final part of the message, expressing views on the most recent German-Polish history (Excerpt):

After a brief independence of about 20 years (1918—1939), the Polish people were overwhelmed, without any blame attaching to themselves, by what is euphemistically called merely the Second World War but which was meant for us Poles as complete destruction and extermination. Over our poor fatherland descended a terrible, sinister night such as we had not experienced for generations. With us, it is known generally as the "German occupation period" and under this name it has gone down in Polish history. All of us were powerless and defenceless. The land was strewed with concentration camps, with the chimneys of the crematoria belching forth smoke day and night. Over six million Polish citizens, most of them of Jewish origin, had to pay for this occupation period with their lives. The leading members of the Polish intelligentsia were simply swept away. Two thousand Polish priests and five bishops (a quarter of the then episcopate) were slaughtered in camps. At the outbreak of the war, hundreds of priests and tens of thousands of civilians were shot to death on the spot . . .

Every Polish family had deaths to mourn. We do not wish to tell the whole of the story so as not to tear open again the wounds which have not yet healed. If we cast our minds back at this terrible night for Poland, it is only because we are now, to some measure, understood, we ourselves, and our present way of thinking . . . We are trying to forget. We are hoping that with time—the great divine Cairos—the spiritual wounds will slowly heal.

After all that has happened in the past—and unfortunately in the very latest past—it can be no wonder that the entire Polish people are oppressed by an elementary need for security and are still gazing towards their nearest neighbours in the West with suspicion. This mental problem is, as it were, the problem of our generation and, God will, it will, and must, vanish with good will . . .

The burden of the conditions is still great on both sides and is increased by the so-called "ticklish matter" of this fact of our being neighbours; Poland's western frontier along the Oder and Neisse is, as is well understand, for Germany an extremely bitter fruit of the last war of mass extermination— together with the suffering of the millions of refugees and Germans who were expelled (which took place by order of the Victor Powers—Potsdam 1945!) . . .

Do not bear a grudge against us, dear German brothers, if we recall what has taken place in the last phase of our thousand-year history. It is intended to be less an arraignment than our own justification. We well know that the consciences of very large parts of the German population were for years at a time subjected to superhuman pressure on the part of the National Socialists; we are aware of the frightful spiritual anguish to which the upright and responsible German bishops were exposed—to mention merely the names of Cardinal Faulhaber, von Galen, Preysing. We know about the martyrs of the White Rose, the resistance fighters of July 20; we know that many

101

laymen and priests sacrificed their lives (Lichtenberg, Metzger, Klausener and many others). As Christians and Communists, thousands of Germans shared the fate of our Polish brothers in the concentration camps . . .

And yet, in spite of all this, in spite of this situation, almost hopelessly oppressed by the past, just because of this situation, we call upon you, Very Reverend Brothers: let us try to forget. No polemics, no further Cold War, but the beginning of a dialogue as is everywhere being striven for by the Council and by Pope Paul VI. If there is genuine good will on both sides—and this we can scarcely doubt— then a serious dialogue must succeed and with time bring forth good fruit—in spite of all, in spite of "ticklish matters" . . .

We beg you to convey our greetings and thanks to the German evangelical brothers who with us and with you are trying to find solutions to our difficulties.

In this wholly Christian, and at the same time very human, spirit we hold out our hands to you there in the benches of the Council that is now drawing to an end. We grant forgiveness, and we beg for forgiveness. And if you, German bishops and Council fathers, grasp our outstretched hand in the spirit of fraternity, then, and not till then, can we celebrate our millennium with a clear conscience here in Poland in a truly Christian spirit. And to join us in the celebration we issue you a warm invitation . . .

December 5, 1965

Reply of the German Bishops to the Polish Episcopate
(Excerpts)

. . . We regard it as a precious fruit of our common work in the Council that you have been able to address these words to us. With gratitude we seize on them and hope that the dialogue started in Poland and Germany can be continued together. With God's help this discussion will promote and consolidate brotherliness between the Polish and German peoples . . .

Terrible things have been suffered by the Polish nation at the hands of Germans and in the name of the German people. We know that we have to bear the consequences of the war, which lie heavy upon our land, too. We realize that the period of the German occupation left behind smarting wounds that can only slowly heal, even with good will. All the more are we thankful that, in view of this, you acknowledge with true Christian magnanimity how in the period of National Socialism the consciences of many parts of the German population were subjected to heavy pressure . . .

We are grateful that, apart from the immeasurable suffering of the Polish people, you are also mindful of the hard fate of the millions of expelled Germans and refugees . . .

So we too beg that one forgets, indeed we beg that one forgives. To forget is a human virtue. The plea for forgiveness is a summons to those to whom wrong was done to see this wrong with the merciful eyes of God and to let a new start be made.

This start is especially burdened by the bitter consequences of the war started and lost by Germany. Millions of Poles had to be resettled from the East into the territories assigned to them. We well know the significance of these territories for present Poland. But millions of Germans too had to leave their homeland in which their fathers and their forefathers had lived. These had not come into your country as conquerors but in the course of the centuries had been summoned there by the resident rulers.

Therefore, we must say to you in love and truthfulness: when these Germans speak of "right to one's homeland", they have—a few exceptions apart—no aggressive intent. Our Silesians, Pomeranians and East Prussians merely wish to say that they feel linked with this homeland, though they know that now a young generation has grown up there which equally regards as their homeland the country from which their fathers were expelled . . .

Christian love always tries to mingle with the cares and distress of the other and so overcome tensions and frontiers. It seeks to wipe out the unspirituality of hatred, of enmity, and the seeking of revenge. It will help towards overcoming all the unhappy consequences of the war in a way that is satisfactory and just to all sides. You may be convinced that no German bishop wishes anything else and will never ask for anything else than the fraternal relationship of both peoples in complete sincerity and honest dialogue . . .

March 25, 1966

German Peace Note

The Federal Government transmits a Note on disarmament and the securing of peace, to the Governments of the East European States as well.

This Note, on Germany's peace policy, stresses the desire of all the German people to live on terms of good relations with their neighbours. Its contents also include the proposal to exchange declarations on a renunciation of force with the East European countries (Excerpt):

The German people wish to live on terms of good relations with all their neighbours, and therefore with the East European as well. The Federal Government has therefore, in numerous ways, tried to improve relations with the States and peoples of Eastern Europe. Even when it is considered that many regard this policy with unfounded suspicion, or even do their best to frustrate it, the results, viewed as a whole, are nevertheless satisfactory; they encourage the Federal Government to continue on this course.

Although the Federal Government is making special efforts to cultivate the relationship with Poland—who of all East European countries suffered the most in the Second World War—it has been possible to make only slight progress here. Though the Polish Government is clearly interested in a lively German-Polish trade, it has not so far given any signs that it sets any store on an understanding between the two peoples. Rather, it is making the cultural contacts we seek more difficult, championing the continuance of the partitioning of Germany, and at the same time calling upon the Federal Government to recognize the Oder-Neisse Line, although, as is universally known, the settlement of the frontier questions is postponed, in accordance with the Allied agreements of 1945, up to the conclusion of a peace treaty with Germany as a whole and that, as long as no other frontiers are recognized by a freely elected all-German Government, Germany continues, under international law, to exist within the frontiers as they were on December 31, 1937.

When the Poles and the Germans eventually discuss the frontier in the same spirit that has led to a settlement between Germany and her Western neighbours, then Poles and Germans will also come to terms, since, in this question, neither passion nor solely the power of the victor must decide; here, reason must prevail.

April 28, 1966

Polish Reply to the Federal Government's Peace Note

In its reply to the Federal Government's Note of March 25, 1966, the Polish Government denies that the German offer has any real value as long as the Federal Republic continues her policy of non-recognition of the Oder-Neisse frontier (Excerpt):

... The frontier along Oder and Neisse is final. It was laid down at the Potsdam Conference by a Resolution of the Victor Powers in the name of the anti-Hitler coalition and with Poland's views taken into account. This decision, which represents an act of historic justice, was set in force immediately through, among other things, the implementation of the Resolution on the resettlement of the German population out of the western and northern areas regained by Poland.

As far as a peace conference is concerned, it would only—as is obviously to be seen from the Potsdam Agreement—have to record the formal confirmation of Poland's western frontier.

This frontier cannot be a subject of discussions or of any bargaining and thus a subject of claims on the part of the Federal Republic of Germany. For this reason, there is no problem of frontiers. On the other hand, there is a problem of peace in Europe, since the territorial claims of the Federal Republic of Germany constitute a threat to peace.

2. Similarly, peace is threatened by the attitude of the Federal Republic of Germany towards the German Democratic Republic, which finds expression in a policy of non-recognition of and enmity towards this State . . .

5. In view of the assertion contained in the Note that Poland is allegedly displaying no interest in an understanding between the Polish and German peoples, the Polish Government would like to state yet again that this does not correspond with reality.

Today, the German nation is living in two German States—in the German Democratic Republic and in the Federal Republic of Germany.

With the German Democratic Republic Poland is linked not only by a treaty but also by close friendship and cooperation.

106

The Government of the People's Republic of Poland has demonstrated its good will for normalizing its relations with the Federal Republic of Germany on many occasions. However, the Government of the Federal Republic of Germany, which in its Note asserts that it is making "special efforts" towards developing relations with Poland, is basically pursuing a policy that jeopardizes the possibility of any understanding.

The extent of the present relations between Poland and the Federal Republic of Germany results from the policy of the Government of the Federal Republic of Germany and its attitude towards Poland's vital interests. The conditions for a complete normalization will exist when the Government of the Federal Republic of Germany unconditionally recognizes the existing frontier of Poland along Oder and Neisse and once and for all renounces all claims to Poland's western and northern territories . . .

December 13, 1966

Government Policy Statement
by Federal Chancellor Kiesinger

In his Government Policy Statement, Federal Chancellor Kiesinger speaks in favour of an improvement in the relations with Germany's neighbours in the East, although only a freely agreed settlement of the frontiers would create the conditions for a lasting and peaceful relationship on a good-neighbour basis (Excerpt):

For centuries, Germany was the bridge between Western and Eastern Europe. We would gladly perform these tasks in our own age as well. We are therefore concerned to improve the relations with our Eastern neighbours, who have the same wish, in all spheres of economic, cultural and

107

political life and also, wherever the circumstances make it possible, to establish diplomatic relations.

Among extensive classes of the German population there is the lively wish for a reconciliation with Poland, whose tragic history we have not forgotten and whose longing at last to live in national territory with secured frontiers we understand better than in earlier times in view of the present fate of our own divided nation. But the frontiers of a reunited Germany can be laid down only in a freely agreed settlement with an all-German Government, a settlement that is to create the conditions for a lasting and peaceful relationship on a good-neighbour basis and approved by both nations.

April 29, 1967

Federal Foreign Minister Brandt on the Frontier Question

At the congress of East German *Land* representations, the Federal Minister for Foreign Affairs, Willy Brandt, deals with, among other things, the frontier question (Excerpt):

We all know what explosive power lies latent in territorial problems in the Europe of today. We shall therefore probably agree that, in view of the inability to realize claims, however well-founded, one must not give way to false hopes. Here, too, the end will finally be on the lines of a balancing of interests.

But in the matter of a peace order it is not just a question of frontiers. It is largely a matter of ensuring that right and justice are not trampled underfoot but are recognized as a basis of the peaceful settlement between the States.

We shall have to continue to concern ourselves patiently with drawing nearer a settlement in a peace treaty with our neighbours. With these efforts towards a just and lasting peace settlement, we shall always have to remain conscious of our responsibility for the interests of our State and our people. This is a duty that remains incumbent on every Government. This is a legitimate national method of acting which we can also expect our Allies to understand. . .

What we hope to reach together is a just solution that is acceptable both to ourselves and to our Eastern neighbours. Let me corroborate this with a saying of the great American Ella Wheeler-Wilcox, which is so reminiscent of Abraham Lincoln that it was mistakenly ascribed to him:

"No question is ever settled
Until it is settled right."

November 3, 1967

Federal Chancellor Kiesinger on the Policy towards Poland

At a Press conference, Federal Chancellor Kiesinger replies to, among other things, a question about the Federal Government's policy towards Poland (Excerpt):

We seek a reconciliation with Poland and—always pointing out that the frontier question can be settled only in a peace treaty with an all-German Government, which, after all, is not only our legal standpoint but also that of our Allies—we seek solutions that can be accepted by both countries. This does not preclude that, for instance, even before such a peace treaty joint considerations can be given to a solution such as is acceptable to both peoples.

January 11, 1968

German Reply to a Polish Proposal on Disarmament and Détente

In an address at the Rhein-Ruhr Club in Düsseldorf, Federal Foreign Minister Brandt deals, among other things, with the ideas put forward by the Polish Foreign Minister, Adam Rapacki, on disarmament and détente and with problems of European security:

In an interview with the newspaper "Trybuna Ludu" published last Sunday (January 7, 1968), Foreign Minister Rapacki cast a retrospective glance at a year of Polish diplomacy. He affirmed that it can be said that the efforts towards achieving a genuine, lasting détente, security and cooperation in Europe have intensified. More and more people in East and West are agreed that one should seek, as the basis for European security, a collective security system that could make it possible to overcome the present division of Europe into antagonistic military groupings.

These are statements and considerations which I can say have been for at least a year a firm component of the policy of the Federal Government. They have found expression not only in Government declarations, speeches and interviews but also in practical politics. Both among our Allies and in the measures and proposals reflecting the relationship of the Federal Republic of Germany with Eastern Europe, the Federal Government is trying to open the way to a lasting and just peace order in Europe by overcoming the East-West tensions. There is, however, one difference: the Polish Foreign Minister Rapacki is burdening his proposals with prior conditions. We impose no prior conditions. Rather, we are convinced that it is a question of matter-of-fact cooperation and a removal of suspicion, and that this can create the prior conditions for solving the problems that now seem incapable of solution.

110

In spite of this, I would like to say that between the proposals of the Polish Foreign Minister and our own there are material points of contact. Just as the Federal Government, so does the Polish Government say that it regards the renunciation of the use of force and the threat of force in mutual relations and non-intervention in internal affairs as a basis—or, as Mr. Rapacki says, as a suitable framework—for a gradual build-up of the all-European security. Ideas may vary as to the way in which this renunciation is effected. What is important is—and in this there seems to be no fundamental difference between the Polish Government and us—that the already valid general renunciation of force by all concerned in the East-West relationship should be renewed and thereby specifically related to this relationship.

Just as the Federal Government, so does the Polish Government—according to what its Foreign Minister says—see in a worldwide treaty for preventing the proliferation of nuclear weapons a means of consolidating peace, particularly in Europe, of facilitating further steps towards détente.

In addition, as was the case with the plans that bear his name and that of Gomulka, Mr. Rapacki has also during the last year several times proposed the conclusion of regional agreements aimed at first freezing and then abolishing atomic armament in as large a zone of Europe as possible. The German Government has submitted a related proposal, namely, the proposal step by step to reduce atomic armament throughout Europe, together with the preservation of the relative strengths, and under effective control.

The Polish Foreign Minister advocates the necessity of a control system for supervising the regional agreements. At the same time this could exercise the function of observation against surprise attacks. We share this view.

Foreign Minister Rapacki has also proposed the uniform reduction of conventional weapons in Europe, to run parallel with the measures in the atomic sphere. This tallies with the Federal Government's efforts towards securing that the massive military confrontation in Central Europe is abolished by a phased and balanced reduction of the Armed Forces on this side and the other side of the demarcation line.

The Federal Government considers it realistic if suitable significance is given to the theme of renunciation of force. This need not, of course, hinder extensive considerations of how to improve security in Europe. In this connection I think it is reasonable—and here too I agree with the Polish Foreign Minister—to assume that, both now and in the future, NATO and the Warsaw Pact are the reliable instruments of our security. Their existence need not obstruct the reduction of armaments.

Thus, there should be no lack of starting-points for an objective discussion. There is one obstacle, however, and it is an artificial obstacle if politically maximalistic standpoints are adopted. This applies to all concerned. Maximalism is an obstacle that should be recognized as such everywhere.

March 2, 1968

Memorandum of the German Catholics on the Polish-German Questions

The "Bensberg Circle" was formed by members of the "Pax Christi" movement in May, 1966. On March 2, 1968, it published a Memorandum on the relations between Germany and Poland, signed by a large number of prominent Catholics (Excerpts):

The signatories to this Memorandum on Polish-German questions speak neither for all Germans nor for all Catholics. They are citizens of the Federal Republic of Germany and they are Catholics. They speak for themselves and for all who are prepared to fall in with their considerations and proposals. Their motive is anxiety about peace. However, peace presumes both the reconciliation of the two nations and a just and mutual adjustment of their relations, approved by both sides . . .

I. Reconciliation

German Catholics are associated with the greater part of the Polish people through belonging to the same Church. This bestows on them a special task: to contribute towards the reconciliation of the Polish and the German peoples. We greatly regret that we have not already much earlier in all openness concerned ourselves about peace with Poland and that we have thereby largely robbed the valuable initiatives of individuals of their effect. This omission oppresses us all the more as, in view of the terrible wrongs done to Poland under National Socialist domination, German Catholicism has not produced the courage and strength to protest in a manner that, over and above all diplomacy and political calculation, would have measured up to the fate of the victims . . .

II. Burdens on the Polish-German Relationship

As against these burdens at present lying on the Polish people there is the loss of the German eastern territories. True, the Victor Powers are formally responsible for this, but, apart from the northern part of East Prussia taken possession of by the Russians, Poles were the executors and beneficiaries of these Resolutions. The factual loss of the

Oder-Neisse territories affected the Germans as a nation. It deprived them of a substantial part of their sovereign territory and their vital cultural and economic area. This national loss particularly affected the onetime inhabitants. They were no more and no less participants in the German aggression and the crimes of National Socialism than the rest of the Germans. Some were forced to precipitate flight; some were expelled at the shortest possible notice. Only a few remained behind and their presence tolerated. The remainder lost their homeland, their belongings and their employment. In the reception areas they had to endure difficult years until they found home and employment. Though they were at least partially compensated materially through the Equalization of Burdens and, in the course of the economic upswing, integrated, through personal effort, in the economy, in society and in the State of the Federal Republic of Germany, statistics show that so far their losses have not been fully made up, and for many this can no longer be effected. We Germans have felt the loss of East Germany as an amputation. The expellees have lost their homeland; they are particularly familiar with the regions of the German East; they love them and their culture, as is still displayed in their lives and their memories. They felt themselves uprooted, and many have not yet lost this feeling. They worry about the historical continuity of their existence, thinking thereby not only of their fathers but also of their grandchildren.

The most serious sufferings were inflicted on the Poles in the period 1939 to 1945, at a time in which the final phase is 23 years ago. The injustice suffered by the expellees started 23 years ago. Not yet have these two burdens become submerged in the past, and thus have not yet faded from direct human experience but are ever present.

It serves neither the reconciliation of the peoples nor the future of their States if they present bills to one another.

114

Rather, it serves peace if each side is concerned not too easily to remember what they would gladly forget. Thus, we Germans will have to tell ourselves that, because of their total aims, because of their inhuman terrorism—coldly-planned, and organized and executed by the State—, because of the degradation and de-segregation of the Poles and because of the devastating consequences, which include the expulsion of the Germans themselves—the crimes committed in the name of Germany against Poland are of such a nature that any attempt to set one against the other reduces one to silence . . .

III. The Problem of the Oder-Neisse Territories

In the case of many Germans, particularly of many expellees as well, the resistance to a unilateral recognition of the territorial circumstances created in 1945 without the cooperation of defeated Germany is rooted not in political obtuseness nor in any aggressive nationalism, but derives from an opinion that can be characterized somewhat as follows. A lasting peace can come about only on the basis of justice, though not if justice is abused. Such an abuse of justice is to be seen in the expulsion of millions of Germans from their ancestral homeland and in the detachment of a substantial part of German sovereign territory, effected unilaterally on the part of the Allies, which have created "faits accomplis" before any settlement in a peace treaty is reached. In view of the existing power position, to legitimate these happenings by an unconditional recognition is no contribution towards peace and reconciliation, since this could not break through the circle of injustice. Rather, a new seat of discord is to be feared through the development of a new German nationalism.

The desire for peace is also evident in this opinion, and its starting-point, that there can be no lasting peace if justice is abused, is generally acknowledged. However, the question is whether justice and right, which lead to peace, can be so regarded, as is the case in this opinion, or whether here there is not perhaps a return to unilateral and exaggerated legal positions which disregard the real relation between justice and peace.

Not one of us can close his eyes to the fact that a people whose political leaders picked a quarrel and lost a war is responsible not only factually but also from the aspect of justice. We cannot escape this liability, which affects the entire German nation, if we seriously desire peace. This includes that, apart from compensation and individual restitution, we have also to accept political disadvantages, and these cannot, in principle, exclude even territorial losses. It requires determination in political negotiations and arrangements which once more establish peace on a just foundation . . .

The recognition of this situation does not signify that our Government should not be concerned to keep the political disadvantages affecting the Germans within bounds as far as possible, although it does signify a double appreciation: that, on the one hand, for every type of peace policy and peace settlement our Government needs a very extensive political room for action which must not be limited beforehand by unilateral legal assertions, and, on the other, after what happened through Hitler's attack and its consequences and through the political constellations with and against Poland, a peace settlement with Poland seems inconceivable without involving territorial loss.

Even if we ourselves subscribe to this viewpoint, it is also necessary to say this to the Poles with absolute clarity. Only in this manner can we counter your widespread—and, in view of what happened, justified—suspicion that our legal reservations and our indication of the provisional nature of the detachment of the Oder-Neisse territories ordered by the Allies at Yalta and Potsdam are meant only tactically in order to restore the old German nation-State within the 1937 frontiers, even with the inclusion of the resettlement of the Poles now living in those territories.

If for us it is a matter of a peace founded on justice, we must state categorically that the Germans do not seek any solution wich would result in fresh injustice, either for the Polish nation or for many Polish citiziens . . .

Because of their historical experiences, Poles and Germans are particularly called upon and legitimated to set to work on the difficult formulation and execution, under international law, of the still-not-secured right to a homeland. Both have undergone active and passive experiences in this field; Poles have expelled and been expelled. They know it or they can know it. But after these experiences, the codification of right to a homeland must be orientated towards a future in which there can be no further expulsion, not even an absolutely final expulsion of the increasing millions of Poles now living in the Oder-Neisse territories. With their repeated declarations of renunication of force for the attainment of political objectives, the Federal Government and the expellees' associations have excluded a forced resettlement of the Poles . . .

For many Germans an appreciation of these contexts is an unreasonable demand, particularly for the persons expelled from their homeland. Their material, spiritual and political existence has suffered a terrible shock. On the other hand, it is precisely they who, because of the solidarity resulting from this experience, are in a position to place themselves more seriously and more realistically in the position of the Poles. There are many expellees who for a long time have regarded their fate as being entangled with that of the Poles. Even in the compatriots' associations, many act in the spirit of reconciliation. In spite of this, the realization of this appreciation means for them that they are

117

giving up material aims so far cherished and continue to discard what once belonged to them: a world their fore-fathers and they themselves created, a world their children and children's children were to inherit and develop. It would be easier for the expellees if they could understand this appreciation, not so much as a renunciation expected of them but as a contribution towards a supranational peace order. This could give rise to a liberating deed truly directed towards the future, releasing not only political energies but at the same time bringing about détente and reconciliation between the peoples. We beg our Polish neighbours to make it easier for the Germans to understand this . . .

IV. Steps towards Reconciliation

Governments do not become "reconciled" towards each other. They conclude treaties that are intended to secure a just and orderly peace. However, all efforts towards the securing of a just peace can be successful only if the peoples seriously seek a reconciliation and thereby create a solid foundation for friendly relations. Our relations must be developed in all spheres covering normal relations between neighbour-States. We do not underestimate the economic exchange that has been under development for a long time already. It is precisely the strengthening of economic interdependence that creates structures securing peace, because they dovetail interests and at the same time lead to human contacts. But that is not enough. What is needed is contact between people from all walks of life. Germans know much too little of Polish culture. It is true that the beginnings of an exchange in this direction are there, but they will not yet suffice for the objective of reconciliation. Here the persons expelled from their homeland have a special task. Apart from this, they and their associations, which quite rightly preserve their cultural heritage, can

118

come to assume the positively historic function of serving the transmission of Polish culture. Such activity would convincingly demonstrate that the Germans are discarding the narrow provincialism of nationalism and the materialism of prosperity, that they are at last seizing the historic possibility—with regard to the East as well—resulting from their geographic situation: to be a bridge.

Certainly the difficulties between the political and social systems make cultural cooperation more difficult, but we suspect that more is possible than now appears to be the case, if only the first and most difficult obstacles are overcome . . .

March 18, 1968

SPD Chairman Brandt on the Oder-Neisse Question

In his report at the SPD party conference at Nuremberg, the Chairman, Federal Foreign Minister Brandt, deals, among other things, with the Oder-Neisse Line (Excerpt):

If at the end of the 1940s or the beginning of the 1950s we had received a peace, we should have had to pay very dearly for it, but today the bill has been virtually settled. We have not been presented with it, and most people have forgotten that the bill for the last war is still unsettled. The instalments on it the German people have already paid are high. The partitioning is a tremendous burden. We have made reparations and restitutions, and to this extent items in the peace settlement have been anticipated.

There are now no longer any frontier problems as far as the West is concerned; there are frontier problems as far as the East is concerned. There is one legal entitlement: this is more than ever the right of our entire nation to self-determination. Such legal entitlements have their significance, but they substantiate no claims which can result in reality.

At any rate, there is a severe handicap on their realization. We know that not even a recognition of the Oder-Neisse Line would by itself result in diplomatic relations with Poland. That too is a reality. It is also a reality that 40 per cent. of the people who are living in those territories were born there, and no one is so bold as to think of a new expulsion. It is a further reality that the German nation wants and needs reconciliation with Poland too.

It wants it and it needs it without knowing when its unity as a State will be achieved through a peace settlement. What is the consequence of this? The consequence is the recognition or the respecting of the Oder-Neisse Line until a peace settlement is reached.

It is a consequence that the existing frontiers in Europe must not be changed by force and that the Federal Republic is prepared to enter into appropriate agreements. All nations should be able to live in the absolute certainty that frontiers will no longer be changed against their will.

This is also the feeling, if I have understood it aright, of our fellow-countrymen who have been expelled from their homeland, whose problems and anxieties I do not forget for one moment.

It is part of the internal recuperation of our nation to say so to one another. It is part of the internal consolidation of the Federal Republic. This task does not yet appear so in the Government policy statement. It has, however, a high priority. It calls for the reconciliation of the generations. It calls for the courage to face up to unpleasant truths. It calls for respect of the opinions of others. It calls for decisions that can accord with conscience.

May 17, 1969

Gomulka's Speech in Warsaw

At an electoral gathering in Warsaw, the First Secretary of the Polish United Workers' Party, Vladislav Gomulka, proposes the conclusion of a German-Polish agreement on the recognition by the Federal Republic of Germany of the Oder-Neisse Line as Poland's final western frontier:

There are no obstacles of a legal nature standing in the way of a final recognition of the existing Polish frontiers by the Federal German Republic. We are ready at any time to conclude such an international treaty with the Federal German Republic.

May 20, 1969

Federal Foreign Minister Brandt before the Society for a Knowledge of Foreign Countries (Gesellschaft für Auslandskunde) in Munich

With respect to Gomulka's proposal, the Federal Minister for Foreign Affairs, Willy Brandt, emphasizes "that we are prepared at any time to enter into discussions with the Polish Government about an exchange of declarations on a renunciation of force inclusive of the frontier problem— as an element of a European peace order. We are prepared to talk.

July 22, 1969

State-Secretary Diehl before the Press in Bonn

The Federal Government's Spokesman, State-Secretary Diehl, makes the following statement before the Federal Press Conference in Bonn:

On July 22, 1969, the People's Republic of Poland is celebrating the 25th anniversary of its foundation. The Federal Government wishes the Polish people, who suffered particularly severely in the Second World War, a happy future in peace and security.

With these good wishes the Federal Government adds the hope that a readiness for understanding on both sides will lead to reconciliation between the German and Polish peoples.

The Federal Government's policy is directed towards helping to find new forms of coexistence among the European nations. A German-Polish understanding would, therefore, serve not only the two nations themselves but also represent a joint contribution towards a better European order.

September 1, 1969

Federal President Heinemann on the 30th Anniversary of the Start of the War

On the occasion of the 30th anniversary of the start of the Second World War, Federal President Heinemann broadcast the following statement over all West German radio and television stations (Excerpt):

My fellow-citizens,

Thirty years ago today, on September 1, 1939, the curtain rose on the awful drama we call the Second World War. Following weeks of conflict with Poland about Danzig and the Corridor, Hitler announced, on that September 1, 1939, in Berlin in the Reichstag before cheering Members tumbling over themselves with enthusiasm, 'the struggle for the Reich's right and security'. Firing was returned at a quarter to six in the morning.

However, in spite of, or perhaps precisely because of, the pact on mutual spheres of influence concluded a few days before between Hitler and Stalin, it was only too obvious that our people had been led into an adventure. Many people all over the country held their breath, full of forebodings. It is no longer necessary to delve into the story of how the Second World War came about. Today, it is all-too-evident.

Ever since the 1920s Hitler had been talking, writing, agitating and inciting to hatred, declaring that for him it was a matter of the solution of the Jewish question and German domination over the neighbouring Slavic peoples as far as deep into Russia. Danzig and the Corridor were only the prelude to the programme of the Greater German Reich, of Germanic masters over so-called Slavic sub-humans. Nor is there any point in speaking about the outcome of the war, even if we do not wish to forget that all over the world more than 55 million people lost their lives in the Second World War. All over the world even more people lost their homeland as expellees and resettlers. From the regions on the other side of the Oder and Neisse and the other parts of Eastern Europe alone, 17 million German people suffered this fate. Nor even yet is the final end of the National Socialist adventure to be foreseen. How much longer are we to remain a divided people over the line in Europe forming the demarcation between the power blocs in West and East? How much longer will Berlin remain an intersected city? When will Europe know an order of peace and exercise its self-reliant function in the world? Not even yet, thirty years after the outbreak of the Second World War, is there an answer to such and other questions. Yet one thing is evident: none of these problems will be solved unless we arrive at a reconciliation with all neighbours and regain confidence in one another.

What to our great satisfaction has been achieved with the former 'sworn enemy' France still remains an unsolved

123

task so far as our neighbours in the East, and especially Poland, are concerned. Poland was the first victim of the 1939 onslaught. Her share in war's toll was no less than six million, seven hundred thousand of whom lost their lives as soldiers; the other more than five million, however, as the victims of deliberate extermination. No matter what the responsible persons in Poland in 1939 may have put forward as arguments for Hitler's actions, and no matter how grievous the fate of our countrymen who in 1945 had to suffer the loss of their homeland beyond the Oder and Neisse, nothing can escape the fact that the state of affairs between Poland and us cannot remain as it is. Here, too, at long last the old rifts must be filled in so firmly that no one can ever carry out another invasion. For this the decisive preconditions must be created . . .

Let us, therefore, on this, the thirtieth anniversary of the day the Second World War broke out, reflect on these two things: we must make a new start between ourselves and our neighbours in the East, especially with Poland; we must counter the scourge of new wars with resolution.

October 13, 1969

Start of the German-Polish Economic Discussions for 1970

In Bonn, discussions start between the Federal Republic of Germany and Poland on economic relations covering 1970.

October 16, 1969

Foreign Minister Jedrychowski on German Television

In an interview on German television, the Polish Foreign Minister, Dr. Stefan Jedrychowski, says that the People's Republic of Poland is ready to discuss with the Federal Republic of Germany *all* questions affecting mutual relations. He says, among other things:

Poland does not approach the question of the normalization of relations with the Federal Republic formally. We take the view that the normalization will be the outcome of a process in the course of which the lasting conditions for a peaceful coexistence, a cooperation of the two countries, will be created.

October 28, 1969

Government Declaration by Federal Chancellor Brandt

In his Government Declaration before the German Bundestag the Federal Chancellor states:

The German people need peace in the fullest sense of this word, with the peoples of the Soviet Union and all peoples of the European East also. We are prepared to make a serious attempt at understanding, so that the consequences of the disaster brought upon Europe by a criminal clique can be overcome.

And in another place: "It (the Federal Government) will have a proposal for the initiation of talks sent to the People's Republic of Poland with which it replies to the remarks made by Vladislav Gomulka on May 17, 1969."

November 21, 1969

Note of the Federal Government to Poland

The Head of the German Trade Mission in Warsaw, Ambassador Böx, delivers at the Polish Foreign Ministry a Note of the Federal Government in which talks on all problems of joint interest are proposed.

November 23, 1969

Interview of the Federal Chancellor with "Zycie Warszawy"

In an interview with the Government newspaper "Zycie Warszawy", Federal Chancellor Brandt emphasizes the Federal Republic's preparedness to initiate negotiations with Poland.

December 22, 1969

Note of the Polish Government in Reply

In a reply to the Federal Chancellor's proposals, the Polish Government declares its preparedness to enter into discussions of this nature.

January 1, 1970

Gomulka's New Year Address

In his New Year address, the Polish Party Chief remarks on the relationship between the People's Republic of Poland and the Federal Republic of Germany and announces that an official exchange of views is to take place between Bonn and Warsaw in the first months of the new year.

January 22, 1970

Visit of the Polish Foreign Trade Minister to the Federal Republic

The Polish Minister of Foreign Trade, Mr. Burakiewicz, visits the Federal Republic at the invitation of the Federal Minister of Economics.

February 4–7, 1970

Start of the Preliminary Discussions between Warsaw and Bonn

In the Polish capital the talks start between Warsaw and Bonn. The German side is represented by the State-Secretary in the Foreign Office, Dr. G. F. Duckwitz; his Polish partner in the discussions is the Polish Deputy Foreign Minister, Mr. Winiewicz.

It is agreed that the talks shall be confidential. In all, there are six rounds of discussions:

from March 9–11, 1970 in Warsaw	(2nd round),
from April 22–24, 1970 in Warsaw	(3rd round),
from June 8–10, 1970 in Bonn	(4th round),
from July 23–25, 1970 in Warsaw	(5th round),
from October 5–7, 1970 in Bonn	(6th round).

May 22, 1970

Journey of CDU Bundestag Deputies to Poland

After a nine-day tour of information through Poland, the CDU Bundestag Deputies Hans Dichgans and Peter Petersen plead for a clarification of German-Polish relations. They set their face against an "isolated formal recognition" of

Poland's western frontier and advocate a settlement embracing all problems existing between the two States—i. e., also the question of the emigrants and the establishment of full diplomatic relations.

June 10, 1970

Communiqué on the Fourth Round of Discussions

At the conclusion of the fourth of discussions between the delegations of Poland and the Federal Republic, the following communiqué is issued:

Within the framework of this round of discussions the delegations have concluded the phase of their exploratory exchange of views and are agreed now to work out formulations for the most important parts of an agreement on the normalization of mutual relations.

June 22, 1970

Journey of the Federal Minister of Economics to Poland

As the first Minister of a Federal Government to do so, the Federal Minister of Economics, Professor Schiller, pays an official visit to the People's Republic of Poland.

June 23, 1970

Agreement on Trade and Economic Cooperation

In Warsaw, a long-term agreement between the Federal Republic and Poland on trade and on economic and technological cooperation in the period 1970–1974 is initialled.

June 25, 1970

Journey of an SPD Delegation to Poland

During a five-day tour of Poland, a six-man Bundestag delegation of Social Democrats have talks in Warsaw with leading Polish parliamentarians in the course of which there is a very frank discussion of all important problems between the Federal Republic and Poland, with efforts made to reach mutual agreement.

At the invitation of the Polish section of the Interparliamentary Union, the group of Deputies, headed by the SPD General Secretary Hans Jürgen Wischnewski, also visited Posen, Danzig, Cracow and Auschwitz.

July 7–9, 1970

Talks on Extending Diplomatic Relations

In Warsaw, delegations of the Foreign Ministries of the Federal Republic and Poland engage in talks on the extension of the competencies of the trade missions.

August 6, 1970

CDU Bundestag Deputies in Warsaw

At the conclusion of a tour of information in Poland, the CDU Bundestag Deputies Philipp von Bismarck and Ernst Müller-Hermann issue a statement about the talks carried out in Warsaw. It runs:

The talks carried out by us in Warsaw, in the course of which pretty well all essential German-Polish problems were touched on, took place in a frank atmosphere. They were marked by great candour on both sides.

We have informed ourselves in detail on the situation in the German-Polish economic relations and are very impressed with the reconstruction efforts made in Poland. We have discussed the many opportunities to intensify trade and particularly to increase sales of Polish products on the German market. In numerous talks there was also an examination of the way in which the economy of the Federal Republic can assist with its technical know-how to speed up the development of the Polish economy. Our talks on German-Polish cooperation in the economic sphere ought to be continued at various levels.

Much time was taken up by the current political problems. We have stressed to our Polish conversation partners that in all sections of the German population there is the earnest desire for a reconciliation with the Polish people. Now that we have been successful in completing the reconciliation with our French neighbour and placing the German-Jewish relationship on a new foundation, the normalization of German-Polish relations is a task that is recognized as urgent on all sides.

We have pointed out that appropriate efforts have already been undertaken by the Federal Governments headed by the CDU/CSU and that particularly after our visit to Poland we attach a significance on its own account to the normalization of German-Polish relations. The reconciliation between Germany and Poland must take suitable account of the overall situation in Europe, although it should not remain overshadowed by other international settlements.

With reference to the declaration made by Federal Chancellor Kiesinger in his day, we have confirmed that there exists complete understanding on the part of the CDU/CSU of the wish of the Poles to live and to develop within secured frontiers.

We have tried, however, to make our Polish conversation partners understand that a German-Polish treaty should be so framed that it can secure a wide approval from both nations. The normalization of relations should be driven forward with a clear purpose, even if it can only succeed step by step. In this connection it is indispensable that the tenets of international law should be respected, although it is also necessary to take the special psychological facts in both countries into consideration.

In this context we have drawn attention to the German partition, the Four-Power responsibility, the Berlin situation, and the claim of all Germans to the right of self-determination.

We have tried to convince our Polish conversation partners what contribution towards overcoming the psychological reservations on both sides can be made by making it easier for frontiers to be crossed. The attempt should be made to give as many people as possible from the Federal Republic and Poland the opportunity to come into contact with one another. This holds good particularly for a more extensive youth exchange. We have suggested that the expellees should be given the opportunity to see their homeland once again.

We are convinced that our talks were interesting and useful for both sides and should be continued.

August 12, 1970

Signing of the Treaty between the Federal Republic of Germany and the Soviet Union

In Moscow, Willy Brandt and Walter Scheel for the Federal Republic and Alexei Kosygin and Andrei Gromyko for the Soviet Union sign the treaty on a renunciation of force and on cooperation.

Article 3 of the treaty reads:

In accordance with the foregoing purposes and principles the Federal Republic of Germany and the Union of Soviet Socialist Republics share the realization that peace can only be maintained in Europe if nobody disturbs the present frontiers.

—They undertake to respect without restriction the territorial integrity of all States in Europe within their present frontiers;

—They declare that they have no territorial claims against anybody nor will assert such claims in the future;

—They regard today and shall in future regard the frontiers of all States in Europe as inviolable such as they are on the date of signature of the present treaty, including the Oder-Neisse Line which forms the western frontier of the People's Republic of Poland and the frontier between the Federal Republic of Germany and the German Democratic Republic.

In the exchange of Notes with the Three Western Powers forming part of the treaty instruments and which the Federal Government has forwarded to the Government of the Union of Soviet Socialist Republics it says:

Since a peace settlement is still outstanding, both sides proceeded on the understanding that the proposed treaty does not affect the rights and responsibilities of the French Republic, the United Kingdom of Great Britain and Northern Ireland, the Union of Soviet Socialist Republics and the United States of America.

The first of the six declarations of intent appended to the treaty, which were signed by both sides, reads:

Agreement exists between the Government of the Federal Republic of Germany and the Government of the Union of

Soviet Socialist Republics that the agreement to be concluded by them on . . . (insert the official designation of the agreement) and corresponding agreements (treaties) of the Federal Republic of Germany with other socialist countries, in particular the agreements (treaties) with the German Democratic Republic (see 6), the People's Republic of Poland and the Czechoslovak Socialist Republic (see 8), form a homogeneous whole.

August 15, 1970

Federal Chancellor's Letter to the Chairman of the CDU/CSU Parliamentary Party

In a letter to the Chairman of the CDU/CSU Parliamentary Party, the Federal Chancellor refers to passages in the Government policy statement dealing with policy towards the East European countries and emphasizes that, beyond the treaty with the Soviet Union, the Federal Government "intends also to conclude contractual agreements with the Governments of Poland and Czechoslovakia".

August 19, 1970

CSU Deputy Höcherl on his Talks in Poland

In a reader's letter to the "Frankfurter Rundschau", the CSU Bundestag Deputy Hermann Höcherl comments on his talks in Poland. The letter reads:

I visited Poland from August 3 to 9 and had the opportunity to talk with certain members of the Government, Deputies and Polish journalists. Since the journey coincided in point of time with the Moscow negotiations, the talks concentrated very quickly on the question of the recognition of Poland's western frontier. I put forward perfectly clearly and in all talks the standpoint of the former CDU/CSU

Governments up to and including the Grand Coalition that the recognition of the final frontiers must be a matter for a peace treaty between the Allies and the Federal Republic.

I was the first member of the CSU to make such a tour of Poland. Naturally I took issue in connection with the prejudices against the CSU and their Chairman Strauss I met with at every step, and repeatedly proposed that they should invite Strauss himself some time in order to carry on the argument with him and to convince themselves that we do not deserve these prejudices. The emphasis of the conversations lay on economic policy. Not a single word was spoken about differences of opinion among the leaders of the CDU and the CSU in the question of the policy towards the East European States. On the contrary, after the visit made by Barzel, Schröder and Kohl to Poland had just been announced, there were repeated references to the fact that among the people around these men, and the same holds good for Kiesinger and Strauss as well, absolute unanimity exists in these questions.

The whole was, therefore, not quite as exciting and sensational as was made out. But all the talks were characterized by a mutual readiness to do everything possible to arrive at a normalization and understanding and, beyond that, to engage in practical cooperation.

September 16, 1970

Four Points on the German-Polish Theme

After a visit of information to Poland lasting several weeks, the SPD Bundestag Deputy Günter Slotta composes the following résumé:

1. The Poles have a great understanding of the Federal Republic's difficult position. They are aware of the common problems of both our nations. They wish to cooperate

peacefully and amicably with all people and all democratic parties in the Federal Republic of Germany. However, they are also aware of the difference between serious political effort and mere verbal declamation. Therefore, a readiness to understand and caution are the two essential components of their political thought.

2. For the People's Republic of Poland the recognition of the Oder-Neisse frontier by the Federal Republic of Germany is an inevitable demand, although even in this question an appreciation of our constitutional position is to be found. They do not doubt that the treaty formula that has to be negotiated with the Federal Republic is seriously meant; nor is there any doubt about the desire for peace of the new Federal Government composed of the SPD and FDP, and Federal Chancellor Willy Brandt in particular enjoys great confidence.

3. In the People's Republic of Poland, complete clarity exists about the importance of family reunion for the people in the Federal Republic. In spite of all problems connected therewith, there is a readiness to settle this question generously and amicably.

4. The imminent initialling and ratification of the "Treaty concerning the Basis for Normalizing Relations between the Federal Republic of Germany and the People's Republic of Poland" can only be a starting-point for a further rapprochement. A number of concrete steps are necessary if the relationship between the two countries and their peoples are to improve via a "normalization". Governments can only create the bases for understanding and friendship; these objectives can be realized only through the individual action of many people. Already a chance presents itself in the near future when Poland sends a large team to the Olympic Games in Munich. At the same time the Poles wish to present a large cultural programme, not only in Munich but in as many towns in the Federal Republic as possible.

October 2, 1970

CDU Deputy with the Polish Foreign Minister

The CDU Bundestag Deputy Richard von Weizsäcker, who is at present paying a visit to Poland at the invitation of the Polish Institute of International Affairs, has a long conversation with the Polish Foreign Minister, Dr. Jedrychowski.

October 3, 1970

Journey to Poland of Social Democrat Parliamentarians

A ten-man delegation of Social Democrat parliamentarians—six members of the Bundestag and four of the Hamburg Parliament—end an eight-day trip to Poland.

In talks with Polish politicians there is a very outspoken and frank discussion of all problems relating to problems between Germany and Poland. In particular, the German delegation touches on questions in the humanitarian sphere, especially family reunion.

The parliamentarians gain the impression that the Polish public is better informed about the Federal Republic than the other way round. It is regarded as gratifying that the great majority of the Polish people wish for the normalization of relations with the Federal Republic of Germany and hope from the conclusions of the German-Polish agreement for the first decisive step on the road to reconciliation.

October 7, 1970

Communiqué on the Sixth Round of Talks

After the sixth round of talks between Messrs. Duckwitz and Winiewicz, the following communiqué is issued:

The delegations continued their exchange of views on questions of interest to both sides and their work on the draft of a treaty concerning the basis for normalizing the relations between the Federal Republic of Germany and the People's Republic of Poland.

It was confirmed that, in view of the progress made in the talks, the Foreign Ministers of the two countries will meet in Warsaw during the early days of November.

It is expected that Federal Foreign Minister Scheel will arrive there on November 2.

October 10, 1970

Agreement on Scientific Exchange

In Warsaw, the German Academic Exchange Service (*Deutscher Akademischer Austauschdienst*) and the Office of Scientific Cooperation attached to the Polish Academy of Sciences sign a Protocol on scientific exchange.

October 15, 1970

Signing of a Trade Agreement between Poland and the Federal Republic

In Warsaw, the Head of the German Trade Mission in Warsaw, Herr Emmel, and the Departmental Chief in the Polish Foreign Trade Ministry, Mr. Strus, sign the new trade agreement between the People's Republic of Poland and the Federal Republic of Germany.

The purpose of this trade agreement, which is backdated to January 1, 1970, and holds good up to December 31, 1974, is to promote cooperation in the economic and technological spheres.

Resolution of the CDU/CSU Parliamentary Party

With one vote abstention, the CDU/CSU Parliamentary Party in the Bundestag passes the following Resolution on the policy vis-à-vis Poland:

1. An important aim of our policy was, and remains, understanding and reconciliation with Poland. This we regard as an essential precondition for the preservation of peace. On both sides, understanding and reconciliation must be based, morally, legally and historically, on truth and an awareness of political reality.

2. We are concerned to intensify the dialogue between the German and Polish peoples. The greater the success in extending mutual knowledge of the culture and the history, the achievements and the real life of the other people, the sooner will the reconciliation of the nations be possible. Anyone distorting the image of the other nation and certain of its groups jeopardizes the reconciliation. For both nations it is necessary and possible to take another look at one another.

Only in this manner is it possible to dispose of the terrible burdens imposed on both peoples as a result of the crimes of the Hitler régime and the subsequent expulsion of the Germans. This would at the same time create the prior condition for extending the scope of common European convictions and good-neighbour relations.

3. In a European peace order that is secured and is based on national self-determination there is room for a lasting settlement and a close cooperation between Germans and Poles, with both nations freely developing. Future European solutions must not be obstructed by the political cementation of demarcation lines and frontiers. Rather, everything

must be done on both sides to make it possible, step by step, to cross them more easily. For this settlement the door must remain open for both nations. Until a freely-agreed lasting settlement is reached, Poland can be sure that the Federal Republic of Germany will respect her present position.

There must be no forestalling, either materially or formally, of the arrangements in a peace settlement, since the entire German people must be free to determine its actions. Premature committals and a unilateral surrender of positions jeopardize the development of the hoped-for settlement.

4. A policy of reconciliation embraces the aim to secure, formally and materially, the human and group rights in both countries. These include, among other things, the right to the free development of personality, the right to the mother tongue, religion and culture, and the right to free movement and free contact with relatives.

Compensation for the persons who have become disabled through medical experiments, now under discussion, should be settled quickly and generously.

5. We advocate the early establishment of diplomatic relations with Poland. We wish for an intensified exchange in contact between members of all sections of the population, particularly young people. This needs the active cooperation of fellow-citizens who have been expelled from their homeland.

6. We will undertake all efforts to promote the trading and economic exchange of the two nations so far as is possible within the framework of our national and European possibilities. In particular, we advocate the extension of trade and more intensive cooperation to establish a German-Polish chamber of commerce as quickly as possible. Its

principal function would be to bring together economic representatives of the two countries and to facilitate the working-out and execution of joint projects.

October 18, 1970

Polish Views on the CDU/CSU Resolution

The central organ of the Polish United Workers' Party, "Trybuna Ludu", expresses the following views on the Resolution of the CDU/CSU Parliamentary Party in the Bundestag of October 15, 1970 (Excerpt):

Although the fact must be borne in mind that the Christian-Democratic Opposition has for the first time announced its interest in the normalization of the relations with Poland in the form of a special Resolution, it cannot be overlooked that the Resolution adheres to the standpoint of that section of the CDU/CSU which has not yet abandoned its policy of placing post-war realities in Europe in question. In its Resolution the CDU/CSU has repeated, with the statement 'Until a freely-agreed lasting settlement is reached, Poland can be sure that the Federal Republic of Germany will respect her present position' its bankrupt thesis of the alleged provisional character of our western frontier. In other words, the fundamental basis for a genuine normalization of relations with Poland, the recognition of the final character of the Oder-Neisse frontier, is rejected. Clearly unmindful of the more sombre experiences of its people's past, the CDU/CSU is still seeking to place in question the frontiers of the Reich that resulted from the unconditional surrender. In this connection the words of the Christian Democratic Resolution with which this party pleads for an 'early establishment of diplomatic relations' has a demagogic ring. How do the Christian Democrats envisage such an establishment of diplomatic relations if the Federal German Republic refuses the most important principle governing the normalization of the relationship with Poland? On the other hand, indignation must be aroused by the efforts of the compilers of the afore-mentioned CDU/CSU Resolution to place the murder of more than six million Polish citizens by German fascists on a level with the resettlement of German people from our western territories pursuant to the Potsdam Agreement concluded by the Victor Powers of the anti-Nazi coalition and carried out under the supervision of the Allies. The CDU/CSU Parliamentary Party's Resolution has met with the approval of the reactionary West German Press. On the other hand, newspapers aware of the need of the Federal German Republic's foreign politics to take the territorial and political realities of Europe into account point out that the Resolution provides a smoke-screen for efforts to prevent negotiations on the normalization of relations between Poland and the Federal German Republic ... The juggling with meaningless verbal statements, the nourishing of illusions on the alleged provisional character of European frontiers—nothing of this helps to create suitable conditions for the normalization of relations between Poland and the Federal Republic: it is the proverbial water on the mill of incorrigible revenge-seekers and opponents of East-West détente who are again screaming between Elbe and Rhine.

October 29, 1970

Initiation of Negotiations with Poland

The Press and Information Office of the Federal Government announces:

"At its session on October 29, 1970, the Federal Cabinet has examined and approved the proposals put forward by the Federal Minister for Foreign Affairs for the conduct of negotiations with the Polish Government.

"In the conclusion of a treaty with the People's Republic of Poland the Federal Government envisages the possibility of placing the relationship between the two States on a new basis, of contributing towards the reconciliation of the two nations and of rendering a substantial contribution towards détente in Europe.

"Before the signing of the treaty the Federal Cabinet will study the results of the negotiations."

November 2, 1970

Federal Foreign Minister Scheel goes to Warsaw

The Federal Minister for Foreign Affairs makes the following statement at the Cologne/Bonn Airport before flying to Warsaw:

Today we shall take a further step towards reaching an understanding with Eastern Europe. In a few minutes we are flying to Warsaw, where difficult negotiations await us. I hope it will be possible to conclude them successfully. I believe there is good will on both sides.

Our negotiations have been carefully prepared. Since last February the State-Secretaries have been studying the material. Formulations have been examined. Agreement on decisive points is still lacking. The vast majority of our people know what it is all about. To create at last the basis for a mutual understanding between the Federal Republic of Germany and Poland is no everyday diplomatic business.

Europe will know no good atmosphere as long as a wall of historic burdens, of mistrust and prejudices exists between the two countries. The German delegation will do what it can, with care and patience, to pull down this wall.

This involves sacrifice. It is inevitable in this hour not to think of those fellow-citizens who must be particularly sensitive to this sacrifice.

We do not press; nor do we feel ourselves pressed. We must, however, now take a decisive step towards initiating normalization between our two countries.

The first journey ever taken by a Foreign Minister of the Federal Republic of Germany to Warsaw is a first step on this road.

After announcing the arrival of Federal Foreign Minister Scheel and the welcome accorded him by the Polish Foreign Minister, Dr. Jedrychowski, at Okecie Airport, Radio Warsaw broadcasts the following statement made by the Head of the Press and Information Department of the Warsaw Foreign Ministry, Mr. Poleszczuk:

The visit of Minister Scheel means that the political talks between Poland and the Federal German Republic have entered a new, important phase. The outcome of these talks is to be an agreement on a treaty for a normalization of the relations between the People's Republic of Poland and the Federal German Republic. Relevant talks have already taken place at State-Secretary level between delegations of the two Governments.

Our official political discussions with the Federal German Republic came about on the strength of the well-known initiative of the First Secretary of the Polish United Workers' Party, Vladislav Gomulka, on May 17, 1969. In this way the discussions have assumed, as a starting-point, the necessity of the recognition by the Federal German Republic of the final character of Poland's western frontiers along the Oder and the Lausitz Neisse. This level can create real foundations for a genuine normalization of relations between Poland and the Federal German Republic.

143

November 3, 1970

First Day of Negotiations in Warsaw

Early in the morning, Federal Foreign Minister Scheel visits his Polish colleague, Dr. Jedrychowski, for a confidental talk by themselves. Questions connected with the treaty are discussed and it is agreed that the negotiations shall be kept confidential.

Later on in the morning the negotiations start with a plenary session of the two delegations. According to the German Government Spokesman, Herr von Wechmar, they are conducted in a matter-of-fact atmosphere appropriate to the significance of the subject.

Herr Scheel takes the occasion to state that the Federal Government regards the development of normal and good relations between the German and Polish nations as a task to which it attaches great importance, because success will denote considerable significance not only for the two nations concerned but also for the future of Europe as a whole.

This is why the Federal Government has entered into these negotiations and the discussions that have led up to them with the earnest wish to do everything possible to facilitate a growing understanding between the two nations and the normalization of relations between the two States.

The Federal Foreign Minister assures that the German side appreciates the fact that the Polish Government and the Polish people regard the frontier question as the central problem of German-Polish relations and realizes that the handling of this question is the key problem to the future relations.

Herr Scheel takes the occasion to summarize the phase of preliminary negotiations and states that in its proposals the Federal Government is proceeding on the assumption that it can undertake commitments for the Federal Republic

only, and that it cannot forestall any all-German representation at an eventual peace conference and that account
must be taken of the rights and responsibilities of the Four
Powers for Berlin and Germany as a whole. Bilateral agreements between the Federal Republic of Germany and the
People's Republic of Poland can neither replace nor antic-
ipate a peace settlement for Germany as a whole.

Nor can, nor should, the frontier settlement, however it
may look, signify a legitimation of those measures as a
result of which millions of Germans have been expelled
from the territories behind these frontiers.

In reply, the Polish Foreign Minister, Dr. Jedrychowski,
states (Summary):

The continuation of the talks at Ministerial level signifies
that these talks have entered a decisive phase. Public
opinion, in both countries and also internationally, shows
that great interest has been displayed in them. Public
opinion expects that on the outcome of the talks will
depend not only the perspectives of the normalization of
relations between Poland and the Federal Republic but
also in no less measure the perspectives of the relations
with the rest of the European continent.

On many occasions the Polish Government has said that
it attaches great importance to the normalization of relations
between the two countries. This accords with the principle
of Poland's foreign policy, which is based on the principles
of peaceful coexistence.

With regard to the normalization of relations with the
Federal Republic of Germany, the Polish Government's
standpoint is based on the readiness to initiate the normalization process between the two countries on the basis of
the recognition of existing realities, especially the final
character of the fixed and existing western frontier of the
People's Republic of Poland.

145

Dr. Jedrychowski states that the policy of earlier Federal Governments has been to question the final character of Poland's western frontier along the Oder and Neisse despite the fact that the frontier had been laid down in the Potsdam Agreement and had been recognized by the German Democratic Republic in the 1950 Görlitz Agreement. The initiative taken by the First Secretary of the Polish United Workers' Party, Mr. Gomulka, on May 17, 1969, was an expression of Poland's standpoint.

Dr. Jedrychowski then goes on to stress that, in relation to the treaty, it has so far been possible in the course of the talks to achieve a narrowing of views, and recalls that in the past the Polish Government has often declared its readiness to normalize relations with the Federal Republic. However, all political initiatives in this direction, as all other Polish proposals for détente in Central Europe, have been rejected by earlier Governments of the Federal Republic.

With regard to the question of family reunion, the Polish Foreign Minister states that this complex of problems cannot be a subject of bilateral agreement since it is a matter of an internal problem of the People's Republic of Poland.

In the evening the Polish Foreign Minister gives a Dinner for his German colleague. He takes the opportunity to make an after-dinner speech in which he says, among other things (Summary):

The presence of the Federal Foreign Minister in his capacity of Foreign Minister, and thereby the visit of a German Foreign Minister to Warsaw for the first time since the war, emphasizes the importance of the meeting. For both delegations the fact that the world at large was showing interest in the negotiations of the two sides was an occasion for undertaking all efforts, in the hope of a peaceful adjustment of relations, to find a way by which

146

a positive and peaceful cooperation between States with different social orders could be developed.

The Polish Foreign Minister states that a complete normalization of relations with the Federal Republic will be difficult without a definite settlement of the most important political questions. He recalls that Poland was the first country to be drawn into war in 1939.

Now, Poland is seeking to establish good relations with the Federal Republic. The prospective treaty can be a corner-pillar of the future relations.

The Minister stresses that it is still the desire of his Government to lay a new foundation for relations in their entirety with the Federal Republic. He is convinced that the good will of both countries will result in a satisfactory conclusion.

Federal Foreign Minister Scheel replies with the following toast (Excerpt):

This delegation from the Federal Republic of Germany has come to you in Warsaw because it wishes to give expression to the conviction of the Federal Government that 25 years after the ending of the Second World War the time is ripe for a settlement between our two countries and the reconciliation of our two nations. We have come in order together with you to negotiate on a treaty that is to end the unhappy past and open out the prospects for a constructive and peaceful future.

You know that the treaty we wish to conclude forms a unified whole with other treaties with East European countries. We are, however, also conscious that the relationship between Germany and Poland is marked more strongly than other international relationships in Europe by the close contact of our two peoples, by the vicissitudes of history, by gladness and sorrow. In the case of the present

147

negotiations, too, we are prepared to take adequate account of this circumstance.

The policy of the Federal Republic of Germany is directed towards a peaceful state of affairs and towards cooperation between East and West in Europe. How is this cooperation possible if we do not succeed in placing the relationship between our two nations on a new basis and in directing our gaze away from the past towards the future?

It was once said somewhere else that the reconciliation between Poles and Germans is of the same historical order as the Franco-German reconciliation after the Second World War. In point of fact there are many similar features in the historical development of these nations. I regard it as a lucky omen that the very day of my arrival in Warsaw I had talks in Paris with my French colleague which, as you know, take place within the scope of a cooperation contractually agreed.

Let us together break through the infernal circle of European history. It has brought our peoples only destruction, partition and sorrow. Let us remember the cultural achievements with which Poland and Germany have enriched the lives of the European peoples. Let us remember our young generation, knocking on the state chancellery doors and demanding account. These young people have only one wish: to live and let live! We who have experienced the Second World War owe it to them not to deny them the chance offered by today.

But let me say one thing in all openness: no treaty however skilfully hatched can replace that element that alone guarantees friendship and security between nations—confidence.

After all that has happened in the past, only slowly can this confidence, on both sides, grow, just as a very sick person can only slowly regain his health. The surest way to accelerate this process is cooperation. Our two nations should measure their strength on works of peace, and then will they recover first the confidence and then the friendship.

November 4, 1970

Second Day of Negotiations in Warsaw

In the morning the German and the Polish Foreign Ministers have another talk by themselves. At the same time the members of the negotiating delegations discuss parts of the treaty instruments.

The Foreign Ministers' conversation is followed by a plenary session, at which there is a discussion about questions closely associated with the treaty instruments. Both sides agree on the institution of a mixed working-group of experts, to be headed by the Directors of the Foreign Ministries of the two countries, Messrs. Zawadski and von Staden.

November 5, 1970

Third Day of Negotiations in Warsaw

In the morning the actual phase of negotiations at the level of the experts starts. The mixed working-group discusses the whole range of problems. Even the first session helps not inconsiderably to go deeper into and clarify the two Foreign Ministers' declarations of principles. According to the statement of the German Government Spokesman, Herr von Wechmar, the atmosphere is good and matter-of-fact.

In the afternoon the working-group reassembles. At the same time, in a third conversation by themselves the two Foreign Ministers continue their consultations.

The same day the Federal Foreign Minister gives an interview broadcast on the Hesse and the West German radio programmes (Excerpt):

Question:

Mr. Minister, would you say that have been able to convince the Polish side in an unambiguous manner that the Federal Government wishes to solve the problem of the Oder-Neisse frontier despite peace settlement reservations and so on, that it does not wish to leave a backdoor open so that some day later on, under other circumstances, the frontier can all the same once more be placed in question? Is the Polish side convinced that we are serious about this?

Answer:

I hope, indeed I am convinced, that the Polish side now holds this view. My conversation with Dr. Jedrychowski has revolved about this point. We cannot and we will not agree with Poland anything that is ambiguous. The exact terms of what we agree here must be absolutely clear, with no allowance made for different interpretations. And I am convinced that the Polish side is also clear about this. However, what can be expected of us we can also expect of the Polish partner to the discussions, and we must expect it of him.

Question:

So that means that there are still, as before, only formal questions to clarify?

Answer:

Actually, it is quite simple. There are certain facts that cannot just be swept aside. In the first place, there is no peace settlement and no one in the whole wide world would allege that there is; there is none. Secondly, as long as there is no peace settlement the rights and responsibilities of the Allies of the last war exist. They cannot be nullified until there is a peace settlement. They exist, and they continue to exist; no one can curtail them or set them aside. Thirdly, the Federal Republic of Germany can make a declaration about Poland's western frontier on behalf of herself, and that she will do. And the Federal Republic commits herself on behalf of herself, and of course she commits herself to the fullest extent, not just, for instance, with time limits, on behalf of herself, on behalf of the Federal Republic of Germany. If this is seen as it is, then an agreement in this sphere is possible. However, that is not the only sphere we have to discuss; there are many other problems. After all, we want in the last analysis to conclude a treaty that does not depict, and once again definitely establishes in a treaty, this state of affairs as Europe displays them, but we want to conclude a treaty that constructs on the state of affairs as we find them, that accepts them as existing without discussing how they came about or the legal character, that constructs on them and now shapes the future. That means, in the future there are many questions to settle, and yet the treaty we want to conclude, the arrangements as a whole, ought nevertheless to be a starting-point for a normalization, for an improvement in the relations, of the two countries.

Question:

So that means that it is also now a matter in the conversations of both sides becoming clear about how they imagine the process of normalization, the process of the coexistence of the two nations?

Answer:

Yes, that is so. And here I must say that our Polish conversation partners have ideas, ideas also about the spheres which are of particular interest to ourselves, spheres in which the Polish Government is wholly free to take the decisions.

Question:

You mean the humanitarian questions of leaving the country?

Answer:

For instance.

Question:

Generally making it easier to cross the frontier?

Answer:

For instance. I consider the definition "becoming easier to cross" a good definition. We must both attach importance to making the frontiers easier to cross. I may say, in parentheses, that if one wants to become clear about this, one must beforehand be in agreement about just where those frontiers are.

Question:

Particularly when they are secure it is, of course, easier to cross them.

Answer:

Yes, and when they are known, when the frontiers are known, and when they are secure, it is possible to speak about much that points to the future, and of course that is what this is all about. And I can say that the Polish partner to the discussions has also developed his own ideas as to how the future is to be shaped. For him, too, the treaty is the starting-point for a normalization of the two countries' interrelationship with an eye to the future.

November 6, 1970

Fourth Day of Negotiations in Warsaw

In the morning the working-group meets. Before and after the meeting the two leaders of the groups have a conversation by themselves. Following the meeting there is a plenary session under the chairmanship of the two Foreign Ministers.

Joint possibilities of resolving certain important points under discussion have been examined. There is not yet complete agreement between the two delegations about these points; nor has it so far been possible to make progress with the agreements—now showing signs—in treaty formulations or agreements on principles. The working-group is given the task of continuing to concern itself with such formulations and agreements on principles.

In addition, consideration is given to questions connected with the normalization of relations between the two countries that is sought by the two sides. The discussions take place in an objective atmosphere.

The same day, the Federal Foreign Minister gives the "Stuttgarter Nachrichten" an interview, in which he says, among other things:

"What we are trying to achieve is a process of recuperation that makes it at long last possible for both nations to arrive at an unbiassed relationship towards one another. We have succeeded in doing this in our relations with France. Both peoples and both Governments are now committed to the promotion of European solidarity. No good atmosphere can develop in Europe if the two sides are not resolved to improve their relations with one another. That is why the German delegation here is doing its very utmost to make this aim of normalization an integral part of the treaty."

153

November 7 and 8, 1970

Journey of the Federal Foreign Minister to Cracow and Auschwitz

In the afternoon of November 7, Federal Foreign Minister Scheel, accompanied by the Polish Deputy Foreign Minister, Mr. Winiewicz, and other members of the Polish and German delegations, goes to Cracow, where in the evening he visits the royal castle.

On the morning of November 8, he goes, at his express wish, and with a few members of the delegation, to Auschwitz, where he visits the former German concentration camp in which more than four million people lost their lives.

About his visit to Auschwitz the Federal Foreign Minister says:

"The human mind simply cannot comprehend how it is possible for such excesses of inhumanity to take place at all." After a visit there, one understood what it also meant for Poland to be concerned about a treaty on the normalization of conditions.

In the former concentration camp's Visitors' Book Herr Scheel writes these words:

"Faced by this horror . . . it will be our task to preserve the highest values: human dignity and peace among nations."

At noon the Federal Foreign Minister returns to Cracow, where he is entertained at Luncheon by the Chairman of the Municipal Council. He then visits the city's market-place and the Church of St. Mary. In the evening he returns to Warsaw.

At a Press conference in the Polish capital, the Federal Foreign Minister emphasizes that the informal talks he has

154

had during the journey with his Polish partners have done more to deepen an understanding of the attitude, policy and wishes of the others than all negotiations.

November 9, 1970

Fifth Day of Negotiations in Warsaw

In the morning a plenary session of the two delegations takes place. There is a discussion on problems which have a bilateral character and are connected with the process of the normalization between the Federal Republic and Poland.

Later on in the morning the Federal Foreign Minister is received by the Polish Prime Minister, Mr. Józef Cyrankiewicz. The Polish Foreign Minister, Dr. Jedrychowski, and the interpreters of the two delegations participate at the conversation. Mr. Cyrankiewicz takes the opportunity to assure Herr Scheel that it would please the Polish Government if Federal Chancellor Brandt would visit Warsaw if there is a successful conclusion to the negotiations.

In the afternoon both delegations continue their deliberations separately.

At noon Federal Foreign Minister Scheel leaves Warsaw for Bonn, where he informs Federal Chancellor Brandt about the negotiations and tells the Federal Chancellor of the invitation from the Polish Government.

On arrival at Cologne-Bonn Airport, Herr Scheel says:

"We have reached an intermediate phase of the negotiations. Last week saw very intensive deliberations. We have been able to draw closer to one another in a few points, and the weekend in particular has provided an opportunity to carry out intensive discussions with the members of the Polish delegation on details as well. This morning I had a talk with the Polish Prime Minister, who is leaving for

Roumania tomorrow and had asked for a talk with me before leaving. This has again illuminated the motives and backgrounds of the actions of the two negotiating countries, and I hope that this has created a foundation whereby it will be possible this coming week to arrive, for all practical purposes, at formulations we can both accept."

In the evening, in interviews with the Deutschlandfunk and German Television the Federal Foreign Minister describes the state of the negotiations in Warsaw and states that above all in the sphere of the humanitarian questions it has not yet been possible for the two sides to find a common ground satisfactory to both sides.

November 10, 1970

Sixth Day of Negotiations in Warsaw

While Federal Foreign Minister Scheel is attending the EEC discussions in Brussels, in Warsaw the working-groups of the delegations of the Federal Republic and Poland are discussing questions still remaining open. The subjects are: the formulation of the article on frontiers, the substance of an exchange of Notes on the theme of the Allied rights and reservations, and the whole complex of the humanitarian questions.

In reference to this, the Polish newspaper "Zycie Warszawy" publishes the same day a commentary entitled "Beginning of a New Chapter" (Actual wording/ Translation):

"For some time, many newspapers in the Federal German Republic have persisted in referring to the complexity and difference in the nature of problems covered by the term 'humanitarian problems'. Does this mean that certain forces in the Federal German Republic are seeking to arouse the impression that in Poland there is the problem

156

of a German minority, and is the attempt being made, through the creation of such an impression, to let such a problem arise?

"It is repeatedly being pointed out that in Poland there never has, and never will be, the problem of a German minority, and we ought not allow such a problem to be artificially created.

"We do not doubt at all the suffering and pain of the people who a quarter of a century ago had to leave their homeland, and yet we cannot be made responsible for this. The blame lies on the Third Reich and the German people, by far the majority of whom supported Hitler. In no case, however, can the resettlement of these people be equated with the murder of six million Poles, with the terrible martyrdom they had to endure in concentration camps at the hands of fascist executioners. There is no common denominator for these sufferings, since they bear a completely different character. The process of the normalization of the relations between Poland and the Federal German Republic—if it is initiated—also demands an appreciation of this fundamental truth by the population of the Federal German Republic with the help of the mass media.

"We are not against the resettlers but only against the political misuse of the fact of their settlement outside Poland.

"Already twenty-five years ago the decision about the final character of the Oder-Neisse border was taken. No one in the Federal German Republic ought to expect any compensation. Our compensation is our readiness to normalize the relations and to start a new chapter in the history of our two nations. And after all that has taken place between us, this is in fact a great deal, even if it is necessary in order to secure peace for the peoples of Europe, including also the population of the Federal German Republic."

On Tuesday the Polish party newspaper "Trybuna Ludu" also publishes an article by K. Malcuzynski on the German policy vis-à-vis the East European countries. The article ends with the following words:

"Those who are now attacking the Brandt Government in the attempt to change the direction of the Federal German Republic's foreign policy destroy the credit Brandt started to secure not only for himself and his Government but also for his country. They are undermining the confidence that is beginning to develop, even inside the society of the Federal German Republic, in a logical process that is necessary and desirable not only for the relations between our countries, not only for the Federal Republic herself, but for the whole of Europe."

November 11, 1970

Seventh Day of Negotiations in Warsaw

Early in the morning Herr Scheel returns to Warsaw.

Later, both delegations meet for a plenary session. The joint working-group reports on its activities in the last two days, following which the Polish Foreign Minister speaks and then the Federal Foreign Minister.

Both Foreign Ministers thank the working-group for the work it has done. Herr Scheel remarks, in conclusion, that he is convinced that not only has certain progress been made in an approximation of the standpoints but that in the course of the negotiations it will be possible to reach a successful conclusion.

After the plenary session both Foreign Ministers meet, at the wish of Federal Foreign Minister Scheel, for a talk by themselves.

In the evening Herr Scheel gives a Dinner in the Hotel Bristol in Warsaw for his Polish colleague, Dr. Jedrychowski, at which he makes the following after-dinner speech:

"Mr. Foreign Minister, Ladies and Gentlemen,

"It gives me very great pleasure to be able to welcome today as my guests such outstanding Party and Government representatives as well as important representatives of the political and cultural life of the People's Republic of Poland and the members of the Polish delegation.

"My incidental stay in Bonn has again made me realize with what attention and great hopes the people in the Federal Republic are in these days looking towards Warsaw. All are conscious that these negotiations represent an attempt to initiate something new and that a successful conclusion of our efforts will lead to a turning-point in the historical development of Europe.

"The public opinion response in the Federal Republic to the desire for reconciliation and understanding with the Polish people has manifested itself in all the signs of progress so far visible in our negotiations. May I take this opportunity to convey the sincere wishes of the Federal Chancellor, with whom I have exhaustively discussed the present state of the negotiations. I have returned with the firm determination to continue along the road of understanding to which an approach has already been made. I am happy to hear that even while I have been away the sincere readiness of both delegations to join together in doing everything possible to remove obstacles and to understand one another's positions has been determined by the spirit of the negotiations, and this makes me confident that we shall be able to put to use the chance offered us of making a new beginning in the relations between our nations.

"Since November 2 the German delegation has been enjoying your generous hospitality. For this, allow me, Mr. Minister, already here today to express a sincere word of thanks to the Polish Government. You have looked after our wellbeing in a magnificent manner and have also facilitated our work through outstanding organization. For us, the pleasant stay in your country is a valuable opportunity to become better acquainted with it. We are learning to understand better its way out of the painful traces of the past and also the development pointing to the future. Now that I have seen here more and more testimonies to the resolute overcoming of the disastrous consequences of the war, I understand all the more your pride in this achievement of the Polish people, an achievement which meets with our unqualified admiration.

"Yesterday, with deep sorrow the world received the news of the death of that great European statesman, General de Gaulle. The significance of this European, who had fought so consistently for the marching-together of the East and West of our Continent with a readiness to understand, was manifold, and I cannot attempt at this place to do honour to this significance. However, I would like to point out that for the people of the Federal Republic de Gaulle is above all a figure symbolizing the ultimate reconciliation between us and our Western neighbours.

"In these days I have already referred several times to the fact that the Federal Government has never left any doubt that it attaches to the task lying before us, of reaching a lasting understanding with Poland, an importance comparable with the Franco-German understanding. Today, since simultaneously with the memory of the great Frenchman who has now died our joint labours, here in Warsaw, continue to form the focal point of public interest in the Federal Republic, the German people are particularly conscious of this fateful parallelism, and their desire to draw nearer the goal of our East-West policy by finding in the East an equivalent to the already-achieved peaceful cooperation with the Western neighbours is particularly evident.

"Since this policy of peaceful cooperation is also in line with the will and the interests of the People's Republic of Poland, I am deeply convinced of the wise sense of our present negotiations, and I therefore also believe that in the course of the next few days we shall succeed in opening the way to an agreement.

"I raise my glass to the prosperity of the proud Polish people, to your health, Mr. Foreign Minister, to you, very respected guests, to the early start to a happy development of the relations between our countries for the wellbeing of a peaceful Europe that has realized that its future lies in cooperation."

In his reply the Polish Foreign Minister, Dr. Jedry-chowski, expresses the conviction that the negotiations can be brought to a successful conclusion. He describes the future treaty as a solid foundation for the normalization of the relations between the two countries, and repeats that the Polish Government will very much welcome a visit by the Federal Chancellor when the work has been completed.

The negotiations themselves continue to be difficult. It is possible to achieve further progress in an approximation of the standpoints even though there is still no agreement on important points. The humanitarian question continues to be a main problem.

In a statement of views, the Polish Spokesman, Mr. Po-leszczuk, refutes reports about the existence of a German minority in Poland, although he allows it to be seen that in the course of a process of normalization a family reunion can be solved "in a suitable manner". The starting-point for this process was the conclusion of the treaty now being sought. One of the questions connected with the normalization was, of course, the facilitation of departure from Poland of a certain number of persons who, for "humanitarian reasons", wished to leave the country for the purpose of family reunion.

A Spokesman of the Federal Government assures that the German delegation has not made use of the concept of a German minority, nor, he says, is this in line with German policy. It was a matter of a "concerted agreement in individual cases" and progress had already been made in this direction in the course of the negotiations.

November 12, 1970

Eighth Day of Negotiations in Warsaw

The negotiations enter the final phase. In the morning the two Foreign Ministers and their Deputies meet and agree about the further course of the negotiations.

A second working-group is constituted. The first concerns itself with the treaty, the second with the humanitarian questions. Both groups are commissioned to make such progress in the substance of the formulations that resolutions can be passed provisionally on the evening of the next day at a plenary session.

In the afternoon at a Press conference in Bonn the German Government Spokesman, State-Secretary Ahlers, states that the negotiations in Warsaw are not yet completed but that the outlook is favourable.

The same day the Federal Foreign Minister gives an interview to the "Nürnberger Nachrichten" which is published on November 13 (Excerpt):

Question:

Can one take it that the talks in Warsaw conform to your timetable?

Answer:

Yes, they coincide with my ideas. I always felt that some time was needed for this difficult complex, which is so difficult because it is not solely a question of a treaty. What is involved is a balancing of interests, which includes more—e.g., the so-called humanitarian problems, which cannot be settled in international treaties. This needs agreements that have to be worked out with quite exceptional care.

Question:

Do you think the anticipated results can also be upheld before the Opposition?

Answer:

Yes. We uphold them, of course, before everybody. We would agree nothing for which we could not answer before the German public with a clear conscience. In the past the Opposition has time after time stated—and even now— that it regards a settlement of our relations with Poland as a particularly difficult problem and that it is prepared to make sacrifices for such a settlement. If we are really to reach a settlement we must discard ideas carefully cultivated up to now. In this case it is not enough to outline political objectives with high-sounding formulations. Rather, together with my partner I have to seek a compromise in order to reach an agreement, to arrive at a treaty. In doing so it cannot be expected that everybody's expectations are fulfilled.

Question:

Will it be a compromise in which the (Christian Democratic) Union is able to concur?

Answer:

Yes.

Question:

Suppose you initial and the Chancellor signs. How much time will it still require for the process of the normalization to commence?

Answer:

One cannot bind oneself to a precisely determined period of time. The treaty is so drawn up that it is not to be the final stroke under a past epoch, but it is to be the initial step towards a new and better phase in the relations between the two nations. That means that the normalization starts with the signing of the treaty. It can even be said that it has, to all intents and purposes, already begun, because even during the negotiations there have been some changes. The whole complex of the humanitarian questions is also an area that cannot be settled and resolved in a day. That will take place only in the future. However, even this part too has a basis with the conclusion of the treaty. I will only add that the normalization of the relations also includes the establishment of diplomatic relations, without my being able to say yet when this will take place. It is clear that the intention exists on both sides. The question is whether in our negotiations we can already name dates for the establishment of diplomatic relations. I would prefer to leave that open.

Question:

In the negotiations so far, have there been any critical phases, and do you expect any in the final round?

Answer:

The negotiations are as a whole naturally critical, because it is a matter of dealing with problems about which there has been no talk for twenty-five years. A great deal has accumulated. On our side ideas which have for many years no longer been realistic have persisted. But the negotiations have always been conducted on both sides so that crises have been avoided, and I hope this will continue to be the case until the end.

Question:

Have there been any differences of opinion among the Western Allies?

Answer:

No, none. We are keeping in close touch with our Allies, and I can say that for their part the Polish diplomats have also remained in close contact with our Western friends. Here it has been possible in the course of time to secure a harmonization of views. Moreover, as for all other European countries the interest in this treaty for the two parties directly concerned—the People's Republic of Poland and the Federal Republic of Germany—is so great that all wish to help towards making this treaty possible.

November 13, 1970

Ninth Day of Negotiations in Warsaw

In the morning the German delegation delivers to its Polish partner to the negotiations a written exposé on the two subjects under discussion (treaty, humanitarian problems) which are to be discussed at the working-party meeting and, in the evening, in the plenary session.

In the morning State-Secretary Frank has a talk alone with the Polish Deputy Foreign Minister, Mr. Winiewicz.

At noon the two working-groups assemble.

Later in the evening the two Foreign Ministers and their Deputies withdraw for a talk. This lasts one hour.

Following this, shortly before midnight the last, and final, plenary session of the two delegations starts, leading early in the morning of November 14 to an agreement on all questions under discussion.

At the conclusion of the talks the German Foreign Minister praises the particular balance of the agreement as a whole and stresses that the treaty ought to be employed as an instrument to initiate a new phase in the relations between the two countries.

For his part the Polish Foreign Minister emphasizes that the treaty is of historic importance for the relations between the two countries. The treaty as a whole should inaugurate the normalization process and help to fill in the rift that had developed in the past between the two peoples and States. The treaty would have a great influence on relations as a whole among the European States and nations.

The atmosphere of the negotiations is described by both Foreign Ministers as objective and cordial. It is agreed to set up a small editorial commission to execute the necessary comparisons of texts and translations by November 18, 1970, the date on which the treaty instruments are to be initialled.

November 14, 1970

Statement by the German Government Spokesman on the Conclusion of the Negotiations with Poland

The Press and Information Office of the Federal Government issues the following statement by State-Secretary Ahlers on the outcome of the Warsaw negotiations:

"The Federal Government is very satisfied with the successful conclusion of the negotiations.

"It is particularly pleased that in long, tough and difficult negotiations, with the preservation of the German legal standpoint, the Foreign Minister has succeeded in initiating a normalization of the German-Polish relations on a con-

166

tractual basis and thereby making a start on the project of effecting an understanding between the German and Polish peoples."

November 14, 1970

Federal Foreign Minister Scheel on the Outcome of the Negotiations

In Munich, Federal Foreign Minister Scheel states before journalists that it is now important to normalize the relationship with Poland in the same manner as earlier the relations with France. The Foreign Minister stresses that the agreement that had been negotiated will not be an agreement "forestalling a peace settlement". He also refers to the significance of the agreement on humanitarian questions and family reunion.

At the FDP electoral conference he emphasizes that it is the task of the responsible post-war generation to have done at last with the past. "This means not only what we say, that we naturally wish to respect the country of the Poles in secured frontiers. It means that we now also act." This the Federal Government had done. Today's foreign policy called for clarity, truth and lucidity; there could be no "jiggery-pokery" with the problems.

November 15, 1970

Commentary of the Polish Government Newspaper

In a commentary on the conclusion of the Warsaw negotiations, the Polish Government organ "Zycie Warszawy" states, among other things, that history teaches that the significance of treaties does not rest on the formulated text but on the vital content enriching them. Poland was following with great attentiveness how the people of the Federal Republic would react to the treaty.

November 16, 1970

Considered View of the FDP

The Bundestag General Secretary of the Free Democratic Party of Germany, J. F. Volrad Deneke, publishes the following article in "Freie Demokratische Korrespondenz":

The treaty between the People's Republic of Poland and the Federal Republic of Germany is of wide-ranging historic importance. A new page has been turned in the history of the two countries which for more than a thousand years have experienced a very special and always tense interrelationship.

The much-chequered and distressing history of Poland has been fatefully bound up with the histories of Russia, Austria and Prussia. It is a history of long international quarrels and great divergencies of interests and conflicts with the neighbours. The partitioning of Poland and finally the "Eastern March" policy of pre-war Germany—a policy of the just as consistent as logical "Germanizing"—poisoned the nations' mutual relationship. The re-establishment of the Polish State in 1919 did not bring this part of Europe the calm it ardently desired. The course taken by the frontier and all problems connected therewith were no good pre-requisites for a stabilization policy in Eastern Europe. In 1920, the Red Army tried to extend the socialist revolution to Poland, popular nationalistic struggles caused no signs of a really convincing desire for peace to appear, and Hitler's living space and racial policy finally led to the re-partitioning of Poland and to unimaginable suffering for the Polish people.

Against this background, certain remarks about the formulations of the Potsdam Conference in 1945 must be made. The conclusions of the "1945 Conference of Berlin"—as the actual description runs—were laid down in a protocol and a summary, the communiqué. From a number of points it was clear that the negotiation partners proceeded on the assumption that a peace conference on Germany would take place in the near future. For example, the President of the United States and the British Prime Minister wanted to advocate in the—as it was thought—imminent peace settlement that the city of Königsberg and the adjacent area should finally go to the Soviet Union. Beyond this, as the then Secretary of State Byrnes said in a speech on September 6, 1946, in Stuttgart, the United States would support a revision of the German-Polish frontier in favour of Poland.

Byrnes said: "However, the extent of the territory to go to Poland cannot be decided until the final agreement about it is reached." There can be no doubt about the mind of the Western Allies also, even if they did not yet arrive at a "firm fixing" of their will.

Since the conference of Teheran the "shifting west of Poland" had stood on the agenda. Not until the Potsdam Agreement was the Oder-Neisse Line included in binding form in the following sentences: "The three Heads of Government agree that pending the final determination of Poland's western frontier, the former German territories . . . shall be under the administration of the Polish State and for such purposes should not be considered as part of the Soviet Zone of occupation in Germany."

Realistically, the expectation is likely to have been that, with a rapid conclusion of peace, the territories on the other side of the Oder and Neisse would have been separated from Germany by a peace treaty before the escalation of the East-West conflict. The question about the German signature in such a case can only be regarded within the overall

169

context of the total collapse after the total war. In view of the situation at the time, is there anyone who will seriously doubt that this would have been the case?

Instead, the historical development during the last 25 years allowed two German States to come into being. The question of a peace treaty with Germany was postponed to the distant future. As a consequence of the Second World War, the greatest changes can have been expected to have taken place in Germany and Poland. Millions of Germans were expelled from their homes in Silesia, East Prussia and Pomerania and, with the shifting west of their ancestral home, millions of Poles had to leave and seek a new—and at first unloved—homeland, uncertain for the individual.

However, a lasting feeling of security could have developed in both peoples.

This can be the case only if the Germans accept that they have lost the war and recognize the realities arising out of it. That can be the case only if the Poles can be certain of their homeland. Only so have both peoples a real chance to secure a lasting peace in Europe with more security for all.

Eminent politicians of the CDU/CSU and spokesmen of the expellees are doing their very best to resist the consequences of the historical development.

Respect for the expellees' spokesmen. Anybody who loves his ancestral homeland has a right to respect rational grounds less than his feelings. And this all the more so as the renunciation of force has long ago become an historic act, and particularly so in the case of these spokesmen of the expellees.

However, the CDU/CSU are faced by a special complex of problems if now they tread the nationalistic road in opposition to the policy vis-à-vis Eastern Europe, whereas their deceased great Chancellor Adenauer was always ready to acquiesce in unnecessary territorial sacrifice in the West for the sake of peace in Europe.

170

After the war started by Hitler had resulted in a loss for the Polish nation of over six million lives—22 per cent. of the population—and a shifting west not wanted by the Poland herself but not revisable, the effect of the following key sentence of the Resolution of the CDU/CSU Parliamentary Party of October 15, 1970, on the politicians in Poland can be imagined: "Until a freely-agreed lasting settlement is reached, Poland can be sure that the Federal Republic of Germany will respect her present position." This is exactly what Poland cannot do; she cannot rely on this without written and binding agreements. The history of Poland justifies no insecured confidence in her Western neighbours and all the more so if this is demanded by politicians who, in Poland's view, are continuing the foreign policy tradition of national rights dating from pre-1914 Germany and the Weimar Republic and are passionately attacking the present policy of détente of the Liberal Foreign Minister Scheel.

The freely-agreed lasting settlement between Poland and the Federal Republic of Germany—not with the present imaginary all-German State—is now taking place. And this respecting of the status quo is an indispensable prerequisite of security in Europe.

Our Yes to the treaty with Poland will also provide for a turning-point in the so-fruitless discussion concerning expulsion. Every expulsion is, and remains, an injustice, and there is, of course, a right to a homeland. This also holds good for the Poles. In the meantime, both in Pomerania and Silesia, as in Bavaria and North Rhine-Westphalia, the children and children's children of the expellees and resettlers have found a second homeland. Here, and there, they also have a right to this *second* homeland.

Why should it not in future be conceivable for the children of the expellees to have them shown, without envy, the farmsteads of their fathers, so that the twinning of towns that has arisen out of the idea of revising history can produce sponsorships under the sign of a will to understand? The twinnings with French towns are a good example.

Now that the difficult work of reconciliation between Germans and Frenchmen has succeeded, it is time at last to complete the reconciliation with the Poles also. In view of the victims of the expulsion, and in view of the suffering inflicted on Poles by Germans, this is a difficult task of great historic importance for both peoples.

In this its importance, the treaty between the People's Republic of Poland and the Federal Republic of Germany goes far beyond the relationship between these two nations. To satisfy German-Polish relations is to overcome one of the most dangerous seats of discord and uncertainty in Europe. This treaty is, therefore, at least of the same stature as the German-Soviet treaty. It occupies a key position in the efforts towards improving and stabilizing security in Europe.

For the first time since the end of the Second World War, with the Moscow and Warsaw treaties the Federal Republic has initiated an active peace policy towards Eastern Europe and has thereby made a start on the complementation and continuation of Adenauer's peace activities with respect to Western Europe.

This policy is, therefore, a prior condition of further West European political integration also. This integration cannot take place as long as our relations with our Eastern neighbours are not clarified. It is one of the absurdities of Germany's post-war history that, of all people, CDU/CSU politicians do not see, or do not want to see, in this policy of the Federal Government the mission inherent in the legacy left by Adenauer. However, the CDU will have to reflect and to decide, in view of the fact that leading CDU politicians also participated very actively in the clear formulation of the ecclesiastical Memorandum issuing a warning to become reconciled.

172

For the first time the opportunity for a new historical epoch in Europe is opening—an epoch of security in East *and* West. This security in Europe is the condition and prerequisite, not to be replaced by any other, for the long road to the unity of Germany and Europe, to a road without armed force and without political pressure. It remains the historical merit of the expellees' spokesmen that they have pointed out to the Federal Government and the Federal Republic this way of renunciation of force through their 1950 Stuttgart declaration. The treaty with Poland is an important step, far too long delayed, towards the fulfilment of the political programme outlined by the spokesmen of the expellees.

November 17, 1970

Invitation to the Federal Chancellor to go to Warsaw

The Polish Prime Minister, Mr. Cyrankiewicz, sends Federal Chancellor Brandt an official invitation to come to Warsaw for the signing of the treaty.

November 18, 1970

The Foreign Ministers initial the Treaty concerning the Basis for Normalizing their Mutual Relations

At noon, in the Palais of the Polish Foreign Ministry in Warsaw, the German and the Polish Foreign Ministers, Walter Scheel and Stefan Jedrychowski, initial the "Treaty between the Federal Republic of Germany and the People's Republic of Poland concerning the Basis for Normalizing their Mutual Relations". The Polish Foreign Minister makes the following statement:

173

Mr. Prime Minister,
Mr. Federal Minister,
Ladies and Gentlemen,

In the name of the People's Republic of Poland and in my own name, I would like to express deep satisfaction at the happy conclusion of the political negotiations which have been conducted between the Government of the People's Republic of Poland and the Government of the Federal Republic of Germany in the light of the initiative taken by the First Secretary of the Central Committee of the Polish United Workers' Party, Vladislav Gomulka, on May 17, 1969, and approved by Federal Chancellor Willy Brandt on October 28, 1969, as well as in the light of the reply of the Government of the People's Republic of Poland of December 22, 1969, to the Note of the Federal Government of November 25, 1969.

As a result of these negotiations we have just initialled the treaty between the People's Republic of Poland and the Federal Republic of Germany concerning the basis for normalizing their mutual relations. The Polish Government is convinced that this treaty constitutes a solid foundation for the normalization of the mutual relations between the two States. With the treaty a final stroke is drawn under the past and at the same time a new epoch is opened in the relations between the two countries and peoples, an epoch which, I am convinced, will be prosperous and fruitful for both sides.

At the same time the treaty is a contribution by our two States towards the consolidation of security and peace in Europe and will promote the normalization of European relations—irrespective of the political and social differences existing among them—based on cooperation, understanding and mutual advantage of the European States.

In the course of the negotiations, agreement was likewise reached on a number of concrete problems associated with the inauguration of the process of normalization once the treaty has come into force. These are intricate problems because they arise out of a particularly trying past. With respect to these problems too, mutual understanding and results have been achieved which, I believe, will help towards the establishment of normal relations between our countries.

Mr. Federal Minister, please accept the good wishes of the Polish Government and my personal good wishes for the Government of the Federal Republic of Germany, for you, Mr. Minister, for State-Secretary Georg Ferdinand Duckwitz, for State-Secretary Paul Frank who is not among us today, and for all members of the Federal Government's delegation whose notable contribution to the achievement that has made it possible for us today to initial the treaty concerning the basis for the normalization of relations between the People's Republic of Poland and the Federal Republic of Germany.

I would at the same time like to express satisfaction that this treaty, which is of great importance for both States, will be signed by the two Heads of Government, Federal Chancellor Willy Brandt and Prime Minister Józef Cyrankiewicz as well as by the Foreign Ministers.

The Federal Minister for Foreign Affairs, Walter Scheel, made the following statement at the initialling of the German-Polish treaty on November 18, 1970:

Mr. Prime Minister,
Mr. Foreign Minister,
Ladies and Gentlemen,

I would like to thank our Polish hosts for the setting they have given to the conclusion today of our treaty negotiations. We appreciate both the fact that you, Mr. Prime

Minister, are present at the initialling of the treaty concerning the basis for the normalization of the relations between the Federal Republic of Germany and the People's Republic of Poland and the tenor of the words you, Mr. Foreign Minister, have just addressed to us.

The Federal Government too regards the treaty we have initialled here today as a decisive step in German-Polish relations in overcoming the distressing past and facilitating the development of normal, friendly relations between our two countries.

In the past weeks and months our two delegations have painstakingly discussed the contents of this treaty and the related texts. Certain formulations have involved a hard struggle. All in all, however, these German-Polish talks and negotiations have at the same time been determined by the intention to take into account the standpoints and concerns of the other partner to the negotiations and to reach agreements acceptable to both sides. These negotiations have been conducted in the conviction that it is a matter of a historic turning-point in the relations between our countries and that, beyond its bilateral significance, the preparation of the ground for a lasting settlement between our peoples is important for the whole of Europe.

I would like to express my particular thanks to the Polish delegation, to you, Mr. Foreign Minister, to your Deputy, Mr. Winiewicz, and to the other members of the delegation for the spirit in which these German-Polish negotiations have been conducted.

A hard struggle still lies before us to secure the approval of this treaty by the competent parliamentary bodies of the Federal Republic of Germany and by the German public. In view of the problems involved in the achievement of a normal and genuine reconciliation between Germany and Poland, I regard this as a necessary process. The Federal Government will continue its policy undeterred, and I am confident that that policy meets with the approval of a large majority of our people.

This will be all the more so if at the same time the clear desire of the Polish Government for the normalization of relations, of which I have no doubt and which for myself has been confirmed by these negotiations, will also be recognizable by the public at large. I would, therefore, be glad if within the framework of the normalization process concrete steps could be achieved as early as possible after the signing of this treaty. I am thinking, in particular, of the complex we have discussed during our negotiations under the concept of humanitarian problems.

Mr. Prime Minister, Mr. Minister, I am confident that the joint efforts we are instituting with this treaty for a more felicitous future for German-Polish relations can be continued with success, if they remain imbued with the spirit of these treaty negotiations.

November 19, 1970

Communiqué on the Session of the SPD Executive Committee

The Executive Committee of the SPD has noted with satisfaction that the Foreign Ministers of the Federal Republic of Germany and the People's Republic of Poland have initialled the treaty between the two States. The Executive Committee thanks Federal Foreign Minister Scheel for his great efforts.

The treaty is no occasion for jubilation. Not only the persons who have been expelled from their homeland but all Germans are conscious of the seriousness that comes to expression here. They must also, however, know that this is the way that leads us forward in the interest of peace, of the nation and of mankind.

In detail, it is stated:

1. A quarter of a century after the end of the Second World War the reconciliation with the Polish people has at last drawn nearer. There is the hope of a new beginning in the mutual relationship between the peoples. If the treaty becomes effective in this spirit, it can achieve the same historic importance for the German-Polish relationship as did the Franco-German reconciliation.

2. When the German-Polish agreement becomes effective it will open out the possibility of family reunion for many people.

3. The Warsaw Treaty forms part of our overall policy coordinated with the Allies. It does not affect bilateral and multilateral treaties earlier concluded by one or other partner.

4. The treaty establishes the hope that economic, scientific and cultural cooperation with the People's Republic of Poland can be intensified in the interest of both nations.

5. The people expelled from their homeland know that no misfortune war and expulsion have brought in their train can be changed by solemn appeals. There can be no talk of recognizing injustice, although there certainly can be of persons expelled from their homeland serving only a policy of peace and understanding.

6. With the signing of the treaty the way will also be opened for the establishment of diplomatic relations.

November 20, 1970

Statement by the Federal Chancellor

Ladies and Gentlemen,
My fellow-countrymen,

The Treaty between the Federal Republic of Germany and the People's Republic of Poland is a moving document for both peoples.

It is to close a dark chapter of European history. It is to open a new one. The time has come to draw a line and start anew.

More than thirty years have passed since the Second World War began with the German attack. The Polish people had to endure untold suffering.

The war and its consequences have imposed infinite sacrifices on both nations, on us Germans too. Now it is a matter of shaping a peaceful future for our two countries and peoples.

Those who have lost relatives, those who have been deprived of their homeland will find it hard to forget. And we others must understand and respect a burden they carry for all of us.

Yet, in this very hour, I must ask those of our countrymen who have been expelled from their native homes not to persist in bitterness but to look ahead to the future.

It means a great deal that many families now have the prospect of receiving in their midst relatives from whom they have been separated for many years, and that it should be possible for them to revisit the birthplaces and graves of their ancestors in their former homeland.

I am in favour of the Treaty with the People's Republic of Poland because it creates the foundation for a peaceful future. It offers us the chance for understanding and co-operation.

To the Polish people the Treaty gives the assurance that they can live within secure frontiers. And as far as we are concerned, it should enable the principle of renunciation of force to be applied in all of Europe.

Only history will tell whether, as we hope, this will mark the beginning of real reconciliation such as, in the West, we have fortunately achieved with our neighbour France.

The Treaty does not of course mean the retrospective legitimation of injustice. It does, therefore, not mean the justification of expulsion.

What we want, a quarter of a century after the war, is to make a serious attempt at putting a political end to the chain of injustice.

And as regards Poland's western frontier: that there can be neither détente nor secure peace in Europe unless—and, by the way, without touching the rights of the Four Powers with regard to Germany—we proceed from the situation as it is, as it has now been for twenty-five years.

It is not that, today, our nation is abruptly required to make a sacrifice. It had to make it long ago as a consequence of Hitler's crimes.

My Government says what most people in this country have been thinking in recent years.

And we can only hope that this will constitute an inspiring step towards a better Europe. A Europe where frontiers will no longer separate.

That is what the young people of our countries expect. We would wish to spare them, if possible, the burden of the past. We want to begin anew, for their sake.

November 23, 1970

Poland's Deputy Foreign Minister Winiewicz on German Television

The Polish Deputy Foreign Minister, Josef Winiewicz, gives the following interview on German Television in the programme "Panorama:"

Question:

Mr. Minister, what does this treaty signify for Poland?

Answer:

If you will allow me to do so, I would like to call attention to two sentences in the preamble of the treaty. The treaty begins with the sentence: "Considering that more than 25 years have passed since the end of the Second World War of which Poland became the first victim and which inflicted great suffering on the nations of Europe . . ." That is the past which we find it very difficult to forget. I would say that it is impossible for us to forget the past. However, the second sentence says: "Conscious that in both countries a new generation has meanwhile grown up to whom a peaceful future should be secured . . ." That is the future. We are looking towards the future, and I believe—from this aspect—Poland accepts this treaty as the basis for securing peace in Europe. Naturally it depends on how the treaty is accepted by the public opinion in your country, and it also depends on how the treaty as a treaty is executed by the two Governments. But we hope for the best. Then we have a situation in Europe we have missed over the last 25 years of uncertainty and the feeling that something should be done to alter and to consolidate the relations between our two countries. I think that here we have a good foundation for the future, and it is—I would like to say—an advantage for both countries from which both countries and both nations can profit and also the whole of Europe. That is what we are expecting from the treaty.

Question:

Mr. Minister, you have carried out the negotiations. From your earlier statements it would seem that twenty years ago you would have considered it very difficult to imagine yourself sitting with Germans at a conference table and talking about difficult problems?

Answer:

That is true. That was my personal feeling. After all, I first had to attend a German school. I was born before the First World War, although I still feel myself very young, and I never thought it would be possible to strengthen peace in Europe without a good foundation of the coexistence of two nations, a coexistence in such conditions that no one dominates or overwhelms the other country. We believed that a better future could be created between the two countries after the First World War. It proved impossible. Then came the Hitler period; then came the Second World War, with all these experiences we had to endure—and I personally, too. But during the whole time I always thought about German culture, about the great possibilities Germany can give Europe in many a sense. We have realized quite clearly that we must do everything, and I too as politician, to settle our relations not merely with the one German State— and one with which we are living in a friendly cooperation—but also with the second. And therefore it was for me also a personal experience to meet my West German partner at the conference table and seek a way which, as I said at the beginning, must be of advantage to both our peoples and our countries. No one loses, no one gains; both of us must profit. Those are my personal feelings.

Question:

Are you satisfied with the way you have found?

Answer:

Yes. You know, after every treaty one must naturally reflect over a great deal. From our standpoint the treaty could still be better; but if there is a compromise which can be accepted by public opinion in both countries, then it is good.

December 3, 1970

The Federal Cabinet Approves the German-Polish Treaty

The Federal Cabinet agrees unanimously to authorize the Federal Chancellor and the Federal Foreign Minister to sign the German-Polish treaty on December 7 in Warsaw.

Previously—as announced by the Federal Government Spokesman, State-Secretary Ahlers, before the Federal Press Conference—the Federal Foreign Minister had once again explained and justified the treaty in precise detail. Herr Ahlers also stated the following (Excerpt):

In the discussion the Federal Chancellor and the Foreign Minister have emphasized the following:

1. That the treaty is to serve the understanding with the Polish nation and the normalization and improvement of the relations between the Federal Republic of Germany and Poland.

2. That it opens the way for a solution of the humanitarian problems.

3. That it is an important foreign political contribution towards a European peace system and a subsequent settlement of the German problem.

4. That the treaty is in conformity with the Constitution because it neither contradicts the summons in the Preamble to reunification nor anticipates the formation of the political will of a future all-German sovereign State.

In this connection the Federal Chancellor has expressed the hope that, up to the ratification debate, it will be possible to create in the Federal Republic a political climate in which the assessment of the treaty free from political party limitations and political emotions is possible. The Government parties would do everything possible to help to create this climate.

In the discussion the Federal Chancellor has again stressed that everybody knows how painful this treaty will be felt by many, particularly by many of the people who had been expelled from their homeland. It was now, however, a matter of looking towards the future. The Foreign Minister had added that it was a question of the moral obligation to avoid conflicts in the future.

Meanwhile the problem of the course of the frontier brought up again by Herr Strauss was also touched upon. I would like again to repeat what I said at my last Press Conference: The German-Polish treaty relates to the existing frontier, and this exists quite independently of the former historical events and is covered by the corresponding formulation of the Potsdam Agreement, which in Article I of this treaty is accepted, and with the words "immediately west of Swinemunde".

December 4, 1970

Motion of the CDU/CSU about the German-Polish Treaty

The CDU/CSU Parliamentary Party moves the following Motion in the Bundestag:

I. The German Bundestag affirms that an important aim of German policy is understanding and reconciliation with Poland. It sees in the attainment of this goal an essential prerequisite for the securing of a lasting peace in Europe. On both sides, understanding and reconciliation must be based, morally, legally and historically, on truth and a sense of political reality.

In a European peace order that is secured and based on the self-determination of nations there is room for a lasting settlement and close cooperation between Germans and Poles, with both nations freely developing.

Anyone desiring this settlement must keep the way open for future European solutions. At the same time he must be prepared to dispose of the terrible burdens that were imposed on both peoples through the crimes of the Hitler régime and the expulsion of the Germans.

II. The German Bundestag begs understanding of the Polish people and all European neighbours for its duty and

184

determination unreservedly to adhere to the right of the German people to free self-determination and to a freely-agreed peace settlement for Germany as a whole.

The final definition of the German frontiers can take place only in connection with this peace settlement. Its foundation must be the right of Germans to secured freedom and unity.

This settlement must neither turn back nor halt the wheel of history. It must do justice to the historic and political situation of both peoples. It must serve the development of a Europe in which frontiers no longer divide nations, but make their peaceful coexistence and contacts possible.

III. For the period in which the partition forced upon the German exists, the German Bundestag desires contractually agreed relations between the Federal Republic of Germany and the People's Republic of Poland. Starting from the Oder-Neisse Line, and with reservation to a settlement for the whole of Germany on the basis of self-determination in a peace treaty, this treaty should create a modus vivendi. It should embody the following elements:

1. Obligations binding in international law for the settlement of all contentious questions by exclusively peaceful means. In particular, renunciation of all use and threat of force now and in the future.

2. Free contacts between people from all walks of life. Binding and concrete settlements of all humanitarian questions aimed at the formal and material securing of the rights of persons and groups (on the lines of the European Convention on Human Rights) in both States. These include the right to the free development of personality, the right to one's mother tongue, the right to the free exercise of religion and cultural activity, and the right to free movement and free intercourse with relatives.

3. Creation of a German-Polish youth organization.

4. Increased exchange in the spheres of culture, art and science. Extension of trade and more intensive technological and economic cooperation. Institution of a German-Polish chamber of commerce.

5. Establishment of full diplomatic relations, within the scope of which the Federal Republic of Germany also represents West Berlin.

December 5, 1970

Announcement of the Head of the German Red Cross Tracing Service

In a talk with the "Rundschau am Sonntag", the Head of the German Red Cross Tracing Service, Dr. Wagner, announces that the Polish Government is prepared to allow the departure from Poland of Germans at an accelerated rate. The German Red Cross is immediately to inform the Polish Red Cross of hardship cases for priority in handling to be given. This also holds good for Germans wishing to emigrate who have no relatives in the Federal Republic.

This operation is to be concluded by the end of 1972. In respect of nationality, the following criteria have been agreed: Which language is spoken in the family?—Who were the parents of the persons desiring to leave Poland?—Which school was attended up to 1945?

The German Red Cross has been expressly informed by the Polish side that applications for departure can also be made by persons who have been declared "Poles" after 1945 or have made such declaration in recent days.

**Statement made by the Federal Chancellor
before leaving for Warsaw**

I am flying to Warsaw to sign tomorrow, together with
Foreign Minister Scheel, the treaty with Poland. The purpose of this treaty is to initiate a normalization and an
improvement in the relations between the two States.
There is more, however, to it than that. This treaty concludes a calamitous chapter of European history that was
filled with great suffering for the nations. It is both an end
and a beginning. It is also this because it makes it possible
for many thousands of people still living in Poland and
wishing to come to Germany to return. Thus, we have been
able to realize a stronger element of humanitarianism in our
policy.

Even if this treaty gives no cause for celebration, we can
nevertheless be satisfied that here a step is being taken for
the organization of peace in Europe.

The following personalities accompany the Federal
Chancellor on the journey to Warsaw:

The Bundestag Deputies Dr. Carlo Schmid (SPD) and
Dr. Ernst Achenbach (FDP) and Professor Dr. Jochen
Frowein, Bochum University; Günter Grass, writer;
Siegfried Lenz, writer; Klaus von Bismarck, Head of the
West German Radio; Henri Nannen, Chief Editor of
"Stern"; Berthold Beitz, Chairman of the Board of Directors
of the "Alfred Krupp von Bohlen and Halbach Foundation",
Chairman of the Board of Directors of Fried. Krupp
G.m.b.H., Essen; Heinz-Oskar Vetter, Chairman of the
Federal Executive Committee of the German Trade Unions
Federation; Walther Haas, Federal Youth Secretary of the
German Trade Unions Federation; Karl-Heinz Neukamm,
Chairman of the Working-group of Young Protestants of
Germany; Dr. Wolfgang Reifenberg, Federal Head of the

Young Men in the Young German Catholics' Federation; Dieter Lasse, Federal Chairman of the Young German Socialists—the "Falken"; and Elsbeth Rickal, Federal Head of the Young Women in the Federation of the Germans.

December 6, 1970

German Delegation flies to Warsaw

In the afternoon, the members of the German delegation, headed by the Federal Chancellor and the Federal Minister for Foreign Affairs, fly to Warsaw, where they are welcomed by the Chairman of the Council of Ministers of the People's Republic of Poland, Mr. Cyrankiewicz, and other Polish personalities.

In the evening, at Polish invitation, a Dinner for a very small circle of guests is given at Castle Netolin. Those present include, on the Polish side, the First Secretary of the United Polish Workers' Party, Mr. Gomulka, Prime Minister Cyrankiewicz, Foreign Minister Jedrychowski and Deputy Foreign Minister Winiewicz, and, on the German side, Federal Chancellor Brandt, Federal Foreign Minister Scheel, State-Secretary Bahr, State-Secretary Duckwitz and Ambassador Emmel.

As the Federal Government Spokesman, State-Secretary Ahlers, announces later at a Press conference, both sides agree to establish diplomatic relations after the German-Polish treaty has entered into force.

In addition, during the conversation at Dinner, there is discussion of the burdens on and development of German-Polish relations, the question of ratification, the Berlin problem, and the relations of European States among each other.

December 6, 1970

Federal Minister Ehmke on German Television

In the evening, in Bonn, the Federal Minister for Special Tasks, Professor Horst Ehmke, gives German Television an interview in which he says:

For centuries, the history of East Central Europe has been determined by the intercommunication and the antagonism of Slavic and German tribes, German and Polish knights, peasants and citizens. The wide-ranging countryside offers no natural frontier. The settlement areas have always run into one another. After more than 100 years of partition, it was possible only at the beginning of this century for the Poles to build up a State of their own. In those days the frontiers of this State, which intersected and separated the old German settlement areas—the frontiers of Versailles—were regarded by the Germans as forced upon them and unnatural. Finally these frontiers of 1937 were taken by Hitler as an occasion for attacking Poland and thereby unleashing the Second World War. Suffering and mutual injustice have always been present in the common history of the German and Polish peoples. However, according to extent and frightfulness, what took place from 1939 to 1946 cannot be described. At the end of this development there were two nations in this area, bled to death, pauperized, expelled from their own settlement areas. In the East, Poland had lost large areas: Germany had had to surrender almost a quarter of her territory to Poland. Millions of persons who had survived the horror of the war and its attendant circumstances had to set out wandering, had to leave their homeland.

All this now lies twenty-five years back. In the meantime the people have found employment and sustenance at the new places where they live. They have married, brought up children, buried the aged. This holds good for Poles and

Germans in like manner. And yet in these twenty-five years we have not learned to seek anything common. We still persist in gazing back at the past and at the injustice that has been done. We reflect on it with bitterness and pain. Anyone who has personally experienced this history and suffering must have a profound respect for the sentiments that are moving us, particularly those of the expellees.

And in spite of this we must look forward into the future. Our children demand from us a world ensuring them a secure life. Old suffering and old injustices have their place in history. They must have no place in the present, and still less in our common future. The time must come when there is no more presenting of accounts. However, how can this be done better than by stretching out one's hand to the other people, the other nation, by making a new start forward? This is the profound meaning of the treaty that is being signed in Warsaw.

This treaty does not prevent us from thinking with pride, gratitude and certainly with melancholy of all that German people have accomplished in cultural, technological and human effort throughout seven centuries in Pomerania, in Mark Brandenburg, in Silesia, in East and West Prussia and in my own city, Danzig. Königsberg, Breslau and Stettin and the lovely spreading countryside between Oder, Neisse, Vistula and Memel linger in our history and in our memories as unforgettable German land. But now, and in the future, they belong to Poland. This may be a bitter realization. There is nothing we can do to change it. And anybody who believes he is able to change it, or even get young people to expect such a change, is playing with war. But we want peace. And for the sake of this peace and the future of our children we are prepared to learn from the painful past, darkened by injustice, and to start a new, peaceful chapter in the common history of the German and Polish peoples.

190

Index of Persons and Subjects

195